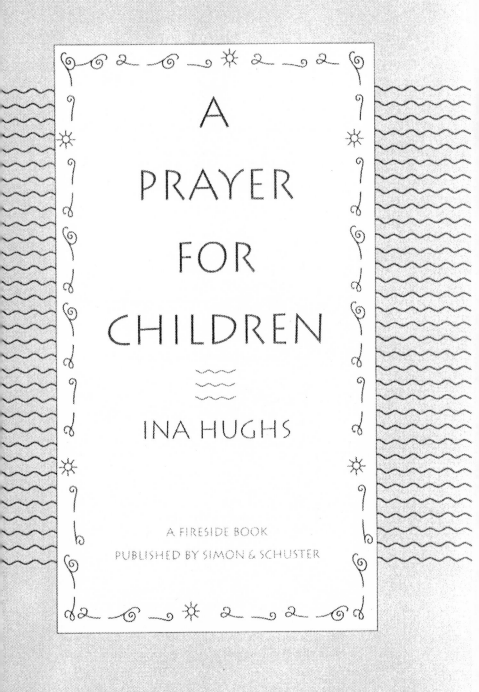

A PRAYER FOR CHILDREN

INA HUGHS

A FIRESIDE BOOK
PUBLISHED BY SIMON & SCHUSTER

FIRESIDE
Rockefeller Center
1230 Avenue of the Americas
New York, NY 10020

First Fireside Edition 1997
Published by arrangement with
William Morrow & Company, Inc.

FIRESIDE and colophon are registered trademarks of Simon & Schuster Inc.

Designed by Chris Welch

Manufactured in the United States of America

1   3   5   7   9   10   8   6   4   2

Library of Congress Cataloging-in-Publication Data
Hughs, Ina.
A prayer for children / Ina Hughs. — 1st Fireside ed.
        p.   cm.
        "A Fireside book."
Originally published: New York : W. Morrow, c1995.
1. Child—Case studies.   2. Child psychology.   I. Title.
                [HQ769.H824   1997]
305.23—dc21   96-39944
                        CIP
            ISBN 0-684-82993-2

Almost all of the pieces previously appeared in slightly different form in
The Knoxville News-Sentinel or *The Charlotte Observer.*

Several pieces were previously published in Ina Hughs' *A Sense of Human,*
copyright © 1993 by The Knoxville News-Sentinel Co., Knoxville, Tenn.

CONTENTS

_—9_

CONTENTS

MINE

OURS

CONTENTS

INTRODUCTION

—෧

There have been lots of studies done on what distin-
guishes human beings from other animals. The fact that we
are different is so obvious, a person can make up his or her
own list off the top of the head:
  We are the only animal that blushes.
  We are the only animal that cooks our food.
  We are the only animal that paints our face.
  We are the only animal that kills for sport.
  And so on.
  But we are not the only animal that cares for its young.
Most animals in the natural world are born with instincts
that echo through millions of years, tracing a common bond
with ancestors that evolved and branched off from those first

creatures that swam, crawled, flew, and finally walked upright. An expectant mother running her fingers over the soft flannel of a crib sheet or sniffing the new-baby smell of powders and lotions; a couple juggling the budget to make room for a college fund; a new father off to the drugstore to buy film—it is all part of something that began millions of years ago and worked itself through time. Written on our DNA is a nesting instinct inherited from our earliest ancestors, some of them now extinct.

One of the hardest "facts of life" discussions I ever remember having was the morning I heard a five-alarm scream coming from my daughter's bedroom, setting in motion the "mother lion" in me. I went racing to the rescue, only to find her white-faced and hysterical, eyes glued in horror at what was happening inside her gerbil cage.

They had eaten their own babies.

Try explaining that one to a six-year-old.

We humans have been given the mental and spiritual equipment to outdo other species in blessing and nurturing our children. Our brains have been fine-tuned to the point that we should automatically put their needs, their welfare above our own. But that's not all. The human heart is big enough to accommodate other people's children as well, to see that not only are we responsible for flesh of our own flesh, but for all children, in all places. As long as one child anywhere suffers—be it Rwanda or across town or sitting next to us at church—it shames us all.

We don't eat our babies, as gerbils do, but sometimes

we exploit them. We forget them. We abuse them. We rationalize and explain them away. Sometimes, we hush them up or pass them off or forget that they are the real measure of any success, be it a family's or a nation's. When we do this—whether we are parents, politicians, preachers, or simply talking over a cup of coffee at the office—we slip a notch on the animal-vegetable-mineral chart. There is something gerbil-like in the way we have become immune to facts, figures, even to the faces of children on the nightly news.

I was thinking about all this one Thanksgiving. Here I was, stuffing a turkey and making sure the Sunday clothes were clean, the jigsaw puzzles handy in case it rained, and the backyard raked in case it didn't—and over the television in the other room comes one of those community-service announcements that feature children who need to find foster care. A TV anchor was "selling" this kid, showing him in the playground and walking along a busy street, naming his good points and giving him a chance to show his best side to the camera. There was a phone number to call if I was interested in giving this child love and attention.

There are two kinds of children in the world: the lost and the found; the haves and the have-nots; the blessed and the forgotten; the lucky and the discards.

Having been raised in a Christian home, I had heard many, many times how prayer is the answer to the world's problems. So I wrote a prayer for children in which I tried to put in words the clear picture I saw in my head of the world's children that Thanksgiving as I was getting ready for the holidays.

When The Children's Defense Fund asked to use the poem in its annual report that year, they asked if they could include the phrase accept responsibility for, parenthetically beside the words pray for. At first, I was taken aback by the suggestion, but after thinking about it, I don't think I have ever heard a better description of prayer as I understand it. Saying a prayer is just words. Anybody can do that. Accepting responsibility for it is putting those wishes and dreams, those good intentions and high ideals, into action.

It's the difference between a picture postcard and a visit.

This book is about children. The whole thing is written as a kind of prayer. In it are things I remember from when I was a child myself, and some of the stories are about my own children. I have tried to look at child-related issues, some serious, some not so serious. I write about other children I have known, whose lives are somehow mixed up in mine.

In many ways, we all tell the same story. If we can understand that, then maybe it will be easier to see that we all have a part in each other's stories and therefore share in both the responsibility and the joy of seeing that all children have a chance: yours, mine, those we only see at a distance, and those we don't see at all because they live in the shadows.

Maybe you've heard the one about the woman who

asked her friend, "What color are your preacher's eyes?"

"I don't know," came the answer. "When he prays, he shuts his, and when he preaches, I shut mine."

What children need today are grownups who preach and pray with our eyes open. And our hearts.

The poem that I wrote that Thanksgiving has now been used in schools and churches all over the country. I probably get two calls a week from people about it. It was read during UNICEF's World Summit for Children, has been reproduced in religious magazines and educational journals as well as by human service and advocacy groups. It is the closing piece in Marian Wright Edelman's best-selling book, The Measure of Our Success. *It has been read three times on national television (including twice on* Good Morning America), *reprinted in a host of editorial columns throughout the country, and even found its way into a segment on one of the soap operas. A friend of mine calls it "the poem that will not die." What I hope is that the concern it expresses will never die, because when that happens, we will no longer be* human beings.

A PRAYER FOR CHILDREN

We pray for children
   who give us sticky kisses,
   who hop rocks and chase butterflies,
   who stomp in puddles and ruin their new pants,
   who sneak Popsicles before supper,
   who erase holes in math workbooks,
   who can never find their shoes.
And we pray for those
   who stare at photographers from behind barbed wire,
   who've never squeaked across the floor in new sneakers,
   who've never "counted potatoes,"
   who are born in places we wouldn't be caught dead,
   who never go to the circus,
   who live in an X-rated world.
We pray for children
   who bring us fistfuls of dandelions and sing off-key,
   who have goldfish funerals, build card-table forts,
   who slurp their cereal on purpose,
   who get gum in their hair, put sugar in their milk,
   who spit toothpaste all over the sink,
   who hug us for no reason, who bless us each night.
And we pray for those
   who never get dessert,
   who watch their parents watch them die,
   who have no safe blanket to drag behind,
   who can't find any bread to steal,
   who don't have any rooms to clean up,

whose pictures aren't on anybody's dresser,
whose monsters are real.
We pray for children
    who spend all their allowance before Tuesday,
    who throw tantrums in the grocery store
    and pick at their food,
    who like ghost stories,
    who shove dirty clothes under the bed
    and never rinse out the tub,
    who get quarters from the tooth fairy,
    who don't like to be kissed in front of the car pool,
    who squirm in church and scream in the phone,
    whose tears we sometimes laugh at
    and whose smiles can make us cry.
And we pray for those
    whose nightmares come in the daytime,
    who will eat anything,
    who have never seen a dentist,
    who aren't spoiled by anybody,
    who go to bed hungry and cry themselves to sleep,
    who live and move, but have no being.
We pray for children
    who want to be carried,
    and for those who must.
    For those we never give up on,
    and for those who don't have a chance.
    For those we smother,
    and for those who will grab the hand of anybody
    kind enough to offer.

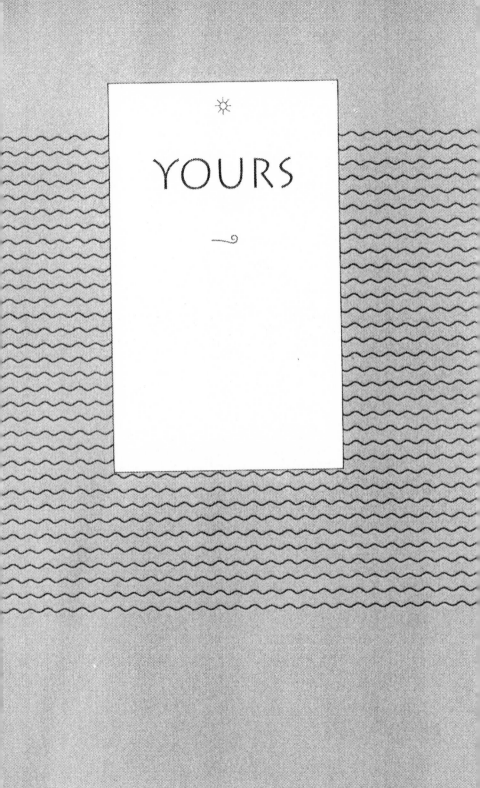

YOURS

The there was the one about the cement mixer who said he liked children in the abstract, but not in the concrete . . .

It's easy to get sentimental or self-righteous when talking about children in general. Maybe if we stopped trying, maybe if we turned that word children into flesh, we would do a better job of taking care of each other. Behind each statistic is a face with a name; within each policy and program are a thousand stories. Maybe our bills and resolutions should have names instead of numbers.

And look at history. Some of its most influential people learned their lessons and touch our lives because of who they were and what they did as children.

You and I are caught up in a common history, and we bump into each other, and each other's children every day. No man is an island, for sure, but in this day and age, we can't even be peninsulas or isthmuses! We're hooked up to each other for life. It sounds impressive to say so, but none of us is really self-made. Life in the twenty-first century won't work on the what's-mine-is-mine principle.

I bet if you stopped to think about the people who have made a difference in your life, you would be surprised at how many children are on that list. Specific children. Some from history. Some living next door. Here are a few of the children mixed in the mortar of my life. I hope it makes you think about those in your own.

PETE

_ᕲ

O nce upon a time, there was a little boy who
didn't like to play basketball. He didn't even like to
watch basketball games. He enjoyed going to basketball games—he just didn't like to watch them.
When the final free throw was being taken in the
last half-second with the score tied, his father would
turn white as a sheet with little beads of perspiration
standing out across his forehead. But this little boy
would look under the seats for more empty Coke
cups to squash.

He had a very fine basketball with a net in the
backyard. He loved to go to the school gym and
squeak his shoes across the court, and every once in

awhile, he passed the time of night away at his homework desk by wadding up spitballs and hook-shooting them into the trash can.

But he didn't like basketball.

One day, his mother was at the grocery store and all she heard about was whose son was on what team at the YMCA. There were car-pool plans and extra practice schedules, and the whole world seemed to buzz with basketball talk. She even saw this one little fellow, couldn't have been more than six years old, walking along beside his mother in tube socks that came up to his chin, and hightop shoes with laces so long, they trailed behind him like a fuse on a land mine. His glitter-gold undershirt, trimmed in black, said he was a Panther. A basketball, which he carried like a lead balloon, kept falling out of his arms and rolling down the aisles, knocking over boxes of cake mix and getting lodged under grocery carts. His mother patted him proudly on the head, explaining that he was the center forward, a real little winner, and he loved playing three afternoons a week and on Saturdays.

You can imagine how this nonbasketball-player's mother felt. After she had loaded her cart with baking soda, vinegar, and red food coloring for the volcano her son was building in the sandbox, she went straight home to talk to him about this basketball thing. She found him stretched out in his beanbag, watching *The Flintstones.*

"How would you like to join a basketball team?"

"Shhh!" Pebbles and Bam Bam were feeding Dino rock soup.

"I saw some of your friends' mothers today, and everybody is playing basketball."

"Mmmmm? Huh?"

"Basketball. Would you like to play?"

"Mmmmm?" Shrug.

"Good."

So it was settled. Or so she thought.

Things went pretty well at first. He came home from school on Mondays and Wednesdays and, mumbling under his breath, went upstairs and put on his purple boxer shorts with the crotch that hung down below his knees, climbed obediently into the back of the station wagon, and polished off a dozen Fig Newtons on the way to basketball.

Out on the courts, he spent most of the time playing imaginary games of ticktacktoe with his feet or counting the iron beams in the rafters. He was great at climbing the goal pole, hopping on one foot all the way across the top bleacher without falling and cracking open his skull—and he was terrific at imitating the buzzer.

Then came the first Saturday game.

"I'm not going," he said.

"Not going? You have to go. You're a part of the team. Everybody goes. You can't be a winner if you don't even go."

"I don't care. I am not going. All week, I work, work, work. I go to school and piano and basketball. Saturday is for fun. Saturday is my day off!"

"Basketball *is* fun."

"I'm glad you like it. *You* go to basketball, and I'll get Dad to take me out to the meat-cutting plant to get me a cow's heart for my science project and then help me fix the wheels on my go-cart. That's what I want to do."

But his mother, being bigger than he, won, and they set off for basketball. On the way, they stopped by the meat department to ask about the cow's heart, and there he waged a final campaign against her by going off and hiding in the shopping center. But a nine-year-old in a shiny purple undershirt, his skinny goose-pimpled legs sticking out from behind a mailbox, is not hard to find.

It was quite a game. His mother screamed until she was hoarse, and nearly fainted when her son, her son! had the jump ball in the final seconds. She didn't even seem to mind that the reason he got the ball was because he had been stuffing the silver wrapping off a stick of gum back in the cover to make a fake piece to give his sister, then suddenly looked up and saw this big kid dribbling down the court, heading straight toward him with no plans of slowing down. His reflexes served him well, and he raised his hands, which happened to hit the ball.

Well, anyway, it was a fantastically exciting game, and all that day she kept telling him, "Good game. Great save."

Later that night he asked her: "By the way, who won?"

"Who won! Why *you* won. Your team won all because of you and the way you stopped the team from scoring that last point. Aren't you proud?"

His face fell.

"Well," he said, "not exactly. I don't really care about winning in basketball, and that guy Jamie, the one who would have scored if he hadn't run into me, loves to win. He said his dad had two bucks on his winning and being the top scorer. Last week, Jamie cried when his team lost. I think the ones who want to win so much and who want to get the ball so much should win. And those of us who don't care should let them. I wish Jamie had scored."

Finally Mom got it.

The shoestrings were taken out of his basketball shoes and used to hang his model helicopter from the ceiling. The purple undershirt was stuffed with newspaper and became the scarecrow in the children's theater rendition of *The Wizard of Oz*. The last time his mother saw the basketball, it was part of the volcano. Every once in a while, she rants and raves about nobody playing with the expensive basketball they bought for him, but it really doesn't matter that much because she knows—she's absolutely positive—that basketball or not, she's got herself a winner.

MELISSA

~๑

She was only eleven. Well, eleven years and five days, to be exact.

Much too young to be scarred for life.

The fancy name for it is *ephelis lentigo*, but most people just call them freckles.

Mom did her best to convince her that freckles were cute. What do moms know? Freckles are freckles, and she had the worst case in recorded history. She was, of course, recording. One hundred and fifty-two at the last count.

She'd believed her dad when he said people improved with age. Like good cheese and savings bonds.

"Hey, look at you!" her grandparents said. "You're growing up, and aren't you pretty?"

"You're in for it with that one," she heard aunts and uncles tell her folks. "Just wait 'til the boys start calling."

Were they blind? Or was that B.F.

Before Freckles.

She hadn't admitted this to anyone, but she was beginning to think about boys and junk like that. Maybe one day . . .

No way. It would never happen. Her phone would never ring. The only way she'd ever know how it felt to be kissed like in the movies was to read *True Confessions* or hear about it at pajama parties. If she absolutely had to have a date for something like her best friend's wedding, she'd have to be fixed up with nerdy sons of family friends—and the only reason they'd agree is because their mothers made them.

Who could fall madly in love with spots?

Maybe she was being punished.

Someone once told her people got a freckle for every lie they told. Had she told 152 lies? I mean, big ones? Big enough to ruin her life?

What would people think if they knew she had freckles on the back of her neck?

Heck, they knew already. The whole world was probably counting them behind her back.

She never used to pay much attention to the face in the mirror when she brushed her teeth. She'd been too busy watching her mouth foam and seeing how close to the drain she could spit.

Now she'd given up such childish ways. No longer did she see through a mirror, dimly. She was, in fact, climbing up on the sink to get a better look.

And all she saw were polka dots.

Old pepper face.

"I look like a dalmatian," she wailed.

Her parents didn't take her crisis seriously. The druggist said there was no cure.

Her brother laughed.

So, she turned to witchcraft. What did she have to lose, besides 152 ways to look ugly? She checked out a book on superstitions, and secretly took the cures one by one.

She rubbed watermelon juice on her face, but all that happened was that she got seeds up her nose.

She tried buttermilk, and the only thing worse than looking spray-painted is looking and smelling like spit-up.

She tried strawberries, dewdrops, positive thinking. And prayer. Lots of prayer.

At last, she gave up. She took the book of superstitions back to the library. She tried to forgive God for being too busy to worry about 152 freckles. Her new approach is distraction: drawing attention away from freckles and on to something else.

Baggy sweaters. Hair in face. Loud socks.

Mom's makeup.

She still hasn't figured out what she did in this life to deserve them. She's still climbing up on the sink to keep a running track, and it was a real setback when she hit two hundred.

Life is tough when you're eleven going on twelve.

Nobody that age ever falls asleep counting blessings. There just aren't that many to go around. Even if you do dig up a few pluses, you have to add the freckles.

Then, subtract.

MARK

It has been more than twenty years since we saw Mark. Then the other night, we showed family movies—and there he was. Same teeth missing. Same cowlicks jutting out the top of his head like antlers on a small deer.

The first time I saw Mark, he was sitting on the front steps of our house in Norfolk, Virginia, talking to the birds. At least, that's what he said he was doing. There weren't any birds around that I could see, but when you are three years old, you don't actually need to have something around just to be able to talk to it.

"Wanna sit on the steps with me?" he asked in a

voice so appealing, it never occurred to me to step over him and take my groceries inside.

Pretty soon, I was chirping right along with him.

Perhaps if I had known what was ahead for all of us who came to love Mark, I would not have turned myself over to him so willingly. When he came by our house for a cookie, he not only got cookies, but all the Kool-Aid and conversation he wanted. Plus all the hugs he could stand.

One of those scenes in our family movies shows Mark coming piggyback across the lawn with my husband "giddyap-ing" silently into the camera. We had no children yet, so it was Mark, you might say, who got that horse warmed up for the thousand rides to come.

I remember so well the day those pictures were taken and how Mark ended up grinning at us forever and ever from around a box of Christmas ornaments.

He and my husband had struck a deal: If Mark would help us decorate our tree, he could have a few branches off it to decorate and put in his room at home.

His folks told us later Mark kept his tree long after all the others in town had been stripped bare and pitched out. When you're four—and Mark turned four that winter—it doesn't have to be Christmas for you to enjoy popcorn and cranberries on the branches of a Scotch pine. Sometime later, he carried his tree out in the back of the garage and fixed a place for the birds to come "wait for each other."

That spring, Mark grew so much, his mother had to add strips of material to his overall straps to lower the hems. By summer, all his pants had patches on the knees, for Mark had discovered he could talk better to the birds if he got up in the trees with them.

By fall, we had moved to Washington, D.C., and kept up with Mark only through an occasional letter from friends.

Shortly before Christmas, we got a letter from Mark's family.

Mark had leukemia.

When we brought in our tree that year, we cut off a little one from the top and put it in the room we were fixing up for our new baby.

By spring, the news was worse, and one night, we got a phone call from Mark's father. They were bringing him to the National Institutes of Health in nearby Bethesda, Maryland. We insisted they stay with us, and the next afternoon, we sat staring at each other in our living room.

Then, jabbering in high-pitched make-believe, we rolled out the sleeping bag and pulled open the sofa bed, like it was all some sort of game. Mark looked so different in his blue baseball cap that he wore all the time because he had already lost most of his hair.

The cap always sat crooked on his head.

The doctors examined Mark and decided if he came to their hospital and lived in a room there and took their strong medicine that maybe—maybe—he would live a few months longer.

Mark's parents rolled up their sleeping bag and gathered up their son and took him home to his yard of trees and birds and his own room.

I don't remember when it happened, but I will never forget how.

When Mark's inappropriate but inevitable time came, his parents once again took him out of the hospital bed with its iron rails and away from the cold, static sounds of doctors being paged, and brought him home.

He died early one morning as he lay in his own bed between his mother and father. The birds were just waking up.

Even after all these years, sometimes when I see a kid with a baseball cap on crooked or hear the birds waking up on an early spring morning, I think about Mark.

And I love him all over again.

HELEN

—๑

Well over a century ago, on the fifth day of summer, a baby girl was born in a two-room farmhouse in Tuscumbia, Alabama. As she was laid in her mother's arms, her eyes squinted against the new brightness of her surroundings.

Perhaps she even heard the family argue over her name.

"Let's call her Mildred," said her father, a former Confederate Army officer and a distant relative of Robert E. Lee.

"No, not Mildred," said her strong-willed mother, who never got far into any conversation without letting on that she herself was an Adams: a

Boston Adams. "She will be named after my mother."

Like all new parents, they stood over their child's crib and counted fingers and toes, listening to the even, easy breathing as they thanked God everything was normal. She grew like a buttercup in the Alabama sun. At six months, her eyes followed her father's strong voice around the room and caught the sunbeams as they fell across her crib.

"I think she'll be a singer," her mother bragged when her little girl turned a year and delighted everyone with a few words warbled out between those wonderful baby noises that do sound like angel songs.

The following summer, they watched her discover the shadow puppets the wisteria vines cast on the front porch and the sound of the guineas scampering across the yard.

"We are so lucky," her mother said as the nights turned warmer and the scratchings of crickets and katydids rose up outside the windows, "because when a baby passes the second summer, she is safe."

But the baby wasn't safe.

". . . acute congestion of the stomach and brain."

That was what the doctor said to explain the tragic turn of events in their daughter's second winter. "She will die."

The doctor was wrong. She didn't die. Her parents thanked God for that, but some of the aunts and cousins whispered that it would have been better if she had, for the fever left the child forever in a silent, black hole.

Deaf. Blind.

The bright-eyed toddler with the angel voice became quiet and sullen. She grew like all children on the outside, but inside, she was locked in a prison she couldn't understand. What had begun as an eager, joyous adventure into life had turned into a frightening, groping battle against the unseen and unheard.

The infinite, ever-present nothingness, the chilling black silence she faced was a strong tide that washed away the small reservoir of memories stored up in her nineteen months of life.

She struck out at this world that had betrayed her, a world that had tempted her with sights and sounds she sought to explore with all the spunk of a bright, curious puppy. That world had taken back its promise and pleasures. In confusion and anger, she sought revenge. She broke things. She wouldn't let anyone touch her, comb her hair, or feed her. She spat at even the tenderest attempts her family made to break through the darkness and find the frightened child who lived inside.

"She's crazy," neighbors said. "Put her away."

But her parents didn't put her away, even though in those days, a person who was blind and deaf was legally considered to be an idiot. On March 3, 1887, when she was six, a special teacher was sent to help her.

"That day," she recalled years later when she was a slight, white-haired woman of seventy, "was the birthday of my soul."

Imagine what it must have been like, that classroom of darkness. To learn what a tree was, she put her cheeks up against it and felt its vibrations. To "see" the rain, she lay in the grass and let it fall on her back. To understand how to count, she felt the six new puppies born to her Belle.

"What is love?" she asked her teacher once. "Why can't I touch it?"

She learned to tell where she was by the smells around her, to identify people by touch, and get to know them by being sensitive to their presence. She got inside things and people in order to understand them.

"I can see colors," she explained once. "White is exalted and pure. Green is exuberant, and red suggests love or shame or strength."

It was amazing that she could learn to communicate by spelling words with her fingers. It was a miracle that she learned to read by feeling dots on a page, opening up for her the world of poetry and Greek mythology through which she moved like a never-tiring traveler.

"How easy it is to fly on paper wings," she wrote.

But, it was impossible that she could learn to speak. No blind and deaf person had ever learned to speak. That fact, she said later, is why she never gave up until she had done the impossible.

"One can never consent to creep when one feels an attempt to soar," she said later, speaking before an audience on behalf of the American Foundation for the Blind.

After graduating *cum laude* from Radcliffe, she set out on a world tour of public appearances. She wrote ten books, received an honorary Doctor of Humanities from Temple University and Doctor of Law from the University of Glasgow. She went on moonlight swims in Nova Scotia, took jeep rides up the cliffs in Portofino, Italy. She fell in love, wrote poetry, told jokes on herself, planted wisteria outside her window, and "saw" Niagara Falls by putting her hands on a windowpane and sensing the thunderous river's famous plunge.

She outlived her parents, her teacher, her doctors. She died in her sleep, napping on the porch beside the wisteria, three weeks before her eighty-eighth birthday. She wrote with her life a textbook for us all, teaching us to forge a path through the darkness—whatever form that darkness takes for each of us.

A reporter once asked her, "Do you believe in life after death?"

"Yes," she answered. "It's like passing from one room to another. Only then, I will be able to see and hear."

Today, Helen Adams Keller is basking in the sun, and not only can she hear the angels, she sings with them.

DAVID

~⌐

The real Romeos of the world are not heavy breathers with capped teeth and a 90210 zip code. They are our kids. Yours and mine. Anybody's. Kids don't need plastic surgery or a lot of practice. They can steal your heart with a sticky kiss or a lopsided grin and never even know it.

Take David, for example. He's four. We met on the playground at his day-care center. He was swinging and talking quietly to himself.

"Want a push?" I asked, a little shyly.

"Sure. If you want to."

One thing led to another, and he invited me up to his classroom. He showed me the paper valentines stuck to the bulletin board and the candy hearts the teacher had hidden in the cupboards.

"We're having a surprise valentine's party," he whispered. "My mama is baking cupcakes."

I asked how he knew—if it was supposed to be a surprise.

"Girls like valentines. My teacher is a girl. My mama is a girl. So?"

He got out a box of plastic geometric puzzles and in no time, had designed a hexagon, a triangle, and figure eight.

There was not enough room for all my parts in the tiny kindergarten chair, and I wasn't sure I wanted to eat the red hots he offered me out of his wet little fist, but, oh! the things we do for love.

"What's this?" he asked, scrambling up the shapes and looking up at me.

I never was very good at geometry.

"I don't know," I mumbled, feeling old and stupid.

"It's a doopy-dangle-do-do-dorgle," he screamed and broke out laughing. Then, balancing a red hot on each finger before he popped it into his mouth, he suddenly got serious: "I've never gone in for Valentine's Day much myself. I like Christmas better. Valentine's Day means you gotta hug and all that junk. I don't really like to hug except my big brother, Keith. I like to hug him."

He pops a blackened red hot into his mouth.

"Keith likes girls, but I'm more interested in pirates. Girls cause problems. Like, sometimes Keith will be playing with me, and he'll have to stop because some girl wants to go to the movies and he has to take her—even though he'd much rather be playing with me.

"Sometimes," he whispers, "girls ask to speak to Keith, and I just hang up!"

With that little secret out, he picks up a lowercase O and hooks it on his nose.

"When I grow up, I might join the marines like my dad wants me to, but I'd rather be an elf."

He waits for my reaction, but I am speechless.

"Don't you want to know why I want to be an elf? Elves get to make toys and take care of reindeer. That's a lot more fun than being a marine, don't you think?"

I asked him what the girl of his dreams would be like.

"I never dream about girls. I dream about pirates!"

Somehow, he realized I wasn't all that interested in pirates, and he took pity.

"Well . . . if I had a girlfriend, she'd have green eyes and red cheeks. She'd have curly hair fixed in those frilly things that hang down on the sides and she'd wear blue flowered dresses."

A movie about winter secrets in the forest was

being shown on the other side of the room. He was out of red hots, and since I was neither a pirate, a reindeer, nor did I have frilly things hanging from my head—he began to wander.

Pretty soon, I'd lost him to Burl Ives and a talking rabbit.

BETTY ANN

—༄

Mistakes.

We all make them. Sometimes, if we're lucky, an eraser will do the trick, and we can rub it across the page, wipe away the dust, and all that's left of our careless mess is a hardly noticeable smudge.

But some mistakes can't be erased. No matter how old or young we are.

I was in the ninth grade the first time I really thought about all this. That year, I learned to diagram sentences on the blackboard, got my learner's permit, wore my first strapless bra, wrote poetry I never read to my parents—but, by far, the toughest lesson I learned was that life doesn't come with erasers. I couldn't make something that had happened, not happen. Even imagination is powerless. There are no erasers. I was fourteen, and I wished then, and I wish now, that I could erase or imagine away what I did, what we all did, to Betty Ann.

She came to our school from Cleveland, Ohio, and to our ninth-grade class in Richmond, Virginia, Cleveland was on another planet.

"Oh, hi! Ohhooo . . ." whispered Margie under her breath as Mrs. Johnson introduced Betty Ann in homeroom that first day. Margie could be real snooty sometimes. Nobody took her too seriously when she got into her rich-kid, old-money mood. She'd entertain us with cruise stories and New York gossip every afternoon as we sat on the front steps after lunch licking the icing off Oreos and begging quarters for a Dr Pepper from the drink machine in the gym. Margie would try to impress us, in her high-pitched, bragging voice, with the *Vogue* models she knew and how they shampooed their hair with beer, that people who ate their whole dinner with their salad fork were not the kind of people her family wanted her to marry into.

Actually, Margie was as insecure and as homely as the rest of us, and her life was about as exciting as the metric system, but we all knew Margie. We all knew everybody. Except Betty Ann. Most of us had been in the same class since kindergarten.

Then came Betty Ann of Cleveland, in her peasant blouses, rolled-down socks, and strange ideas.

If it had been just Margie who dug into Betty Ann, it wouldn't have turned out the way it did; she probably could have handled that. But we *all* were in on it.

I guess what started us off was when Betty Ann wrote a better English composition than Susan Henderson. Susan was the writer of the class, and we were very proud of her. Her weekly story was always so good, Miss Moon usually chose it to read aloud to the class every Friday. Susan would sit back in her desk, a pencil stuck behind her ear, looking to all of us just like a promising young literary genius we could say we once knew.

The Friday after Betty Ann arrived on the scene, Susan twirled her pencil, leaned back in her desk, and waited for the best composition of the week to be read.

Hers, of course.

Only it wasn't. It was Betty Ann's, and it was about a black poet named Langston Hughes and how he had become a spokesman for his people. Susan's stories were always about horse shows or opening nights.

We'd never heard of Langston Hughes. Besides, this was an all-white private school. Martin Luther King was being nailed by most of the adults we knew. All in all, it was a real bomb to have Betty Ann go on about Langston Hughes's "Black Nativity" and his description of the "maple-sugar child" and how he thought Carl Sandburg's poems fall on the page like blood clots of song from the wounds of humanity.

In Susan's stories, the "telephone jangled" and "the rainbow painted the sky." Stuff like that. Betty Ann was writing about the civil war in Spain and the black ghettos of Harlem. Langston Hughes was from Cleveland. We might have guessed.

Mrs. Johnson came to the part in Betty Ann's composition where Langston Hughes writes a poem about how he likes watermelon so much that if he should meet the queen of England, he'd be proud to offer her a piece. That was when Agnes Matherson's eyes caught mine (or was it the other way around?) and we started imitating the queen of England eating a piece of watermelon. The whole class burst out laughing. The rest of the story was never read, and everybody but Betty Ann had to stay after school and clean blackboards. The next day at lunch, Betty Ann found a note under her lettuce saying we were sorry, but the cafeteria was sho' nuf out of watermelon.

After that, she became the class joke. What she wore, what she said, what she ate somehow always gave one of us an idea for a wisecrack. There was a kind of one-upmanship about getting Betty Ann that had less to do with Betty Ann than with our own jungle mentality. I know that now, but I didn't think about it then. She became a pawn.

She started getting sick a lot. There'd be whole weeks when she'd miss school, but the Betty Ann stories went on even without her. She came to our school from another planet. She was our little moron, our Polack, our village idiot.

Then one day, Betty Ann and I were assigned a project together. Everyone had selected a partner, and I was out of town at a school swimming meet the day the assignment was given, so I got stuck with Betty Ann. Everyone kidded me, and I laughed with them. The day before the project was due, I had to go over to her house after school to work on it with her. Her mother fixed a plate of cookies and kept coming into the room to see if I wanted more Coke or anything. She said I was the only one of Betty Ann's friends who had come over after school, and was glad to meet me.

The phone rang while I was there, and it was for me. Betty Ann's mother was in the kitchen when I heard Margie giggling at the other end of the line: "Have you eaten any maple sugar candy or watermelon, kiddo?"

She waited for me to snicker an undercover laugh.

I saw Betty Ann's mother just standing in the kitchen with her back to me, pretending not to be listening. It was as if she had heard everything. I hung up. I think it was at that moment when I began to see what we had been doing.

"Why don't you girls like Betty Ann? She likes you . . ."

Nobody has ever asked me a question before or since that made me feel so stupid.

If kindness could kill, Betty Ann would have been dead in a week. But it was too late. Her parents moved her to another school, then we heard later that she'd had a nervous breakdown.

Once, years later when I was home from college, I saw Betty Ann in the doctor's office. She didn't even recognize me.

Sticks and stones only break bones. Words can shatter the soul. A little, quiet, picked-on ten-year-old runs away because kids on the bus laugh at him. A sensitive ninth grader flips out because a group of self-rising girls decide to throw her to the wolves. We tell ourselves it takes more than that to send someone over the edge. Maybe so. Maybe not.

But there are no erasers.

SAM AND CINDY

_—◡_

Love isn't just blind. Sometimes, it's plain crazy.

Sam was in the fifth grade when love snuck up on him for the first time. He'd slide in the seat next to her in the cafeteria and spit the paper off his straw in her face. He'd forget his math book and have to ride his bike over after school to borrow hers. He even took baths.

His mother only found out because he kept asking for pimento cheese sandwiches in his lunch.

"You hate pimento cheese!" she said.

"I don't eat them," he confessed. "I swap them with somebody."

"Why don't I just make you peanut butter and honey and save you all that trouble?"

"It's no trouble," he said, then he changed the subject.

Mom might not have cracked the case if Little Sister hadn't butted in.

"Sam's got a girlfriend," she said one night at supper while Sam picked at his food. It was a very brave thing to do, because Sam immediately gave her three charley horses under the table. He'd have been better off leaving bad enough alone, because kicking her made Little Sister go one further: "Her name is Cindy and she's the ugliest girl in the whole fifth grade."

At which point Sam slammed his napkin into the middle of his chicken tetrazzini.

"You're dead," he said, flipping a noodle into Bratty Sister's face.

"Cin-n-n-n-d-y," she sang as they were both sent from the table. "Oh, Cindy, my darling . . . *Ouch!* Stop yanking my hair out."

It's a wonder either made it up the steps alive.

Two pimento cheese sandwiches later was Mom's car-pool day. She got there early and watched the children spill out into the yard. There came Sam, dragging his windbreaker behind him and listing slightly to the left.

"My Lord," Mom said out loud. "He's carrying her books."

A diamond ring couldn't have announced it more clearly. Here was a boy who could sit and watch his mother lift sofas with one hand and vacuum with the other; who never batted an eye when she grunted through the den balancing sixteen pounds of laundry on one hip and an aquarium full of algae on the other; a child who went into cardiac arrest whenever he was begged to bring a bag of groceries into the house; and who got so exhausted just brushing his teeth, that he never had the strength to lift the cap off the sink and screw it back onto the tube. Here was that one-in-the-same boy carrying a skinny little spelling book, a couple of spirals, and a science book for a girl who stood a good three inches taller and whose book-carrying arm had more flesh on it than Sam had on his entire body.

But, the real shocker came as they got closer and closer.

Little Sister was right. Shirley Temple, she wasn't. Dirty socks had ridden down in dirty sneakers. Half of her hair was in a pony tail, the other half stuck out as if someone had plugged about six volts of electricity into her ear. She was all legs and teeth, but at least her legs knew which way to go, whereas her teeth didn't.

"Well," Mom said as off-handedly as she could manage when he settled into the seat next to her. "Who was that nice young girl you were talking to?"

"She's just some girl in my class," he said, which meant it had to be Cindy, because he usually didn't speak in complete sentences.

That night, Mom told Dad she had met Sam's valentine.

"What's she like?" he wanted to know.

"It's hard to say. I just saw her from a distance."

"Well?"

"Well, what?"

"Well, anything. Is she tall? Short? Freckles? Is her hair the color of pimento? What sticks out about her?"

"All the wrong things." Mom sighed. "Teeth. Hair. Let's just say that in my heart of hearts, I know there's no such thing as an ugly child, but if there were . . ."

Well, love is blind and makes a person do all sorts of unlikely things—all of which Sam tried to do without attracting too much attention. He bought a box of candy hearts and gave Cindy the ones that said HEART THROB and SECRET PAL. Mom and Little Sister got the ones that said BUG OFF and CREEP. He took the phone into the closet from time to time, dialing her number, disguising his voice and asking her if she liked anyone. He never brought up her name at home, but Little Sister finally got the point that if she wanted a long and healthy life, she'd better not say certain things.

One day, Sam's mom got a call from the school. Sam had been in a fight.

"It wasn't Sam's fault," the principal explained. "A group of children was teasing one of the girls. Sam kind of stuck up for her, and all of a sudden, there was a big fight. Sam got punched good. You'll have to come get him."

That's when Mom learned that love is not only blind. It doesn't make any sense.

"I don't approve of fighting," Mom said on the way home with Sam, whose left eye was turning the color of a pimento. "But, I think it was nice of you to stick up for Cindy like that."

"Stick up for her!" he shouted. "She's the one who beat me up!"

MACKIE

⁓

"Well, you see, there was this vine . . ."

That was her excuse for being thirty minutes late to supper. There was this vine down by the creek where they cut through the new road. A big, delicious vine hanging from a giant oak, swinging ghost-like in the spring breeze over a gurgling creek. A vine, waiting for some little kid to grab hold of it and fly out over the world with a whoop and a holler.

One of the calendar-cover pictures of childhood is a boy or girl gleefully swinging out on a vine, Tarzanlike, with nary a care in the world. But swinging out fifteen feet above the ground, your toes touching the tips of trees and your stomach left back there on the edge of the creek, is not that easy. It looks neat when Norman Rockwell does it, but ask any child who has ever gotten up the nerve. It's not that simple.

You have to reach deep inside to come up with the go-ahead when it's your life on the edge of the cliff.

"Well, you see, there was this vine."

That was the excuse the next night when she was thirty minutes late again. This time, she had a skinned knee and a faint, dirt-stained trail of tears down her cheek. It seems that everybody could go on the big vine. Everybody but her. She was too scared. What if she lost her grip and landed on the rocks in the creek below? What if she lost her nerve halfway across and did something awful like scream out loud in front of her friends, or suppose she let loose and came crashing down in a pile of defeat? What if even one of the little first-grade shrimps who hung back, watching from the sidelines, had the guts to go on the big vine—and she didn't?

So what if the vine was twisted a thousand times around the giant tree, so what if it had been there probably for a hundred years—it just might by some quirk in the law of nature give way with you on it. Accidents happen. Some parachutes don't open. Lightning does strike.

You never know when something might go wrong. You can't be too careful. What if the law of averages and the law of oak-tree roots and vine twisting went bad just as she pushed off, and right there in front of the whole school, everything broke loose?

She would forever be known as the girl who died on the vine.

Hard as she tried, she couldn't keep these thoughts out of her head.

"Well, you see, there was this vine . . ."

A third night she came home late. This time, she'd waited until everybody else had gone, and there on the edge of the creek, she looked fear in the face. Her hands grew sweaty, gripping the vine so tight, it made her fingers throb. She could feel her heart pound, see it make her shirt move as it beat out a drumming warning: *No . . . no . . . no.*

It made her dizzy. Where was her courage? Was she a chicken?

She could do it. It was a cinch. It would be fun. Nobody had been killed. (So far.) Nobody was looking. She took a deep breath. She was going to do it.

But she didn't. At the last minute, she dug her heels into the ground and hung her head and let the tears come.

At night, she dreamed about the vine. She stared at it on the way to school. It almost seemed alive.

Evil, like a snake. There was nobody to whom she could really trust her wildest fears about the vine, nobody who would understand how important it was.

She didn't even understand it herself.

She just knew she had to do it.

Then one night, she comes home, her feet hardly touching the ground, words tumbling out of her mouth in such a crazy order that if you hadn't listened and watched carefully for the past week, you couldn't have imagined what wonderful thing had happened.

"You know that vine down by the creek?" Excitement shoots out of every pore. Words tumble out upside down, backward, and forward. "It's at least a hundred feet high. Could you, please, double-triple-please, drive over with Dad and turn on the car lights and watch?"

You don't say, "Can't we wait until tomorrow?" or ask what happened this time that was different.

You don't ask, because you know.

Somewhere in everybody's past is a vine or a diving board or a rooftop or a swinging bridge—something that just plain haunted the fear away at one glorious moment when you took courage and did it.

It's an important thing to have done, because when the time comes, and it will for us all, when we taste again that fear in our throats as we face an illness or a loss or a change or a wall of fearsome uncertainties, we can remember: "There was this vine . . ."

And we can do it.

ISABELLA

$\sim$

$\int$ ometime during the winter of 1797, two years before George Washington died at Mount Vernon, a black baby girl came into the world with only her mother present in the muddy cellar of Charles Hardenberg's inn in Ulster County, New York.

No one took notice.

After all, the birth of a black female slave was no earthshaking matter.

Her mother was known as Mau-Mau-Bett, and her father, brought over a few years earlier on a slave ship from the Gold Coast, was called Baumfree. Mau-Mau-Bett decided to name her baby Isabella, a Bible name meaning God's oath.

In all her eighty-six years, she never learned to read or write, yet her words are written and her picture found in every history book. She later dropped the name Isabella for another name, not because she was no longer "God's oath," but because the time had come for her to carry out that oath.

When she was nine years old, Isabella was sold at a slave auction for ten dollars and a few sheep. She was healthy and strong and would grow to over six feet. Four years later, she had the first of her five children, all born into slavery.

With the passing of the New York Emancipation Act, Isabella would have been granted her freedom on July 4, 1827. Her fourth owner promised to free her a year earlier for good behavior, and when he backed down on his word, she simply walked out of his house. She was taken in, paid for, and given her freedom by Mr. and Mrs. Isaac Van Wagener. Never having had a last name, she took the name Isabella Van Wagener.

The first thing she did as a free woman was to sue for the restoration of her five-year-old son Peter, who had been illegally sold to an Alabama planter. It was unheard of that a penniless black woman would do such a thing. Who did she think she was?

She didn't think, she knew. Ever since she was a little girl scrubbing floors in Hardenberg's inn, Isabella knew who she was. There was never any doubt in her mind. She knew it when she was eight years old, and she knew it now. She had been sent by God. She was different. Years later, whenever she rose to speak, she began with these words: "Children, I talk to God, and God talks to me."

Together, Isabella and God moved mountains. Peter was returned to his mother, but that was just the beginning.

In 1835, a prominent white businessman who had become involved in a scandal spread rumors saying Isabella had become a free-living, free-loving, self-proclaimed prophet who had tried to poison him. She took him to court. When a white jury awarded her $125 in damages, she became the first black woman to win a slander judgment against the time-honored Goliath of white bureaucracy. People began to notice.

While living in a commune in Northampton, Massachusetts, Isabella became a traffic stopper for the abolition movement. She took on whites and blacks alike. The great black leader Frederick Douglass believed that slave insurrection, not Isabella's spellbinding, nonviolent rhetoric, was the only hope for black emancipation. Douglass called her "low-classed."

"Mr. Douglass reads," she said to her people, "but God himself talks to me."

In 1843, she had a special vision, one in which

God called her to become a wandering evangelist and reformer and to change her name. From then on, she was known as Sojourner Truth.

In an age famous for its orators, Sojourner Truth became one of the greatest public speakers in American history. She spoke on behalf of runaway slaves, of brotherhood and peace, of human rights. She said God was color-blind and that black children were just as much His as white ones, and loved just as much by both their earthly and heavenly parents.

Harriet Beecher Stowe called her the "Libyan Sibyl," saying "Sojourner seems to impersonate the fervor of Ethiopia . . . burning after God in her tropic heart and stretching her scarred hands toward the glory to be revealed."

When the Civil War broke out, Sojourner Truth went to Washington and met with President Lincoln. She helped integrate the Washington streetcars and worked hard to establish settlements for freed blacks in Kansas and Missouri. She helped reunite children taken from their parents and sold off.

Nobody got away with calling her "just a woman."

At the 1851 Women's Convention in Akron, Ohio, the hall fell silent as a white minister preached long and hard against women's rights. Women are frail and delicate, he said. They need to be taken care of by men, because men are stronger and wiser. When he finished, a tall, black woman in a stocking cap and wearing glasses walked proudly to the podium. She was fifty-four years old.

"The man over there says women need to be helped into carriages and lifted over ditches and to have the best place everywhere. Nobody ever helps me into carriages or over puddles or gives me the best place . . . and ain't I a woman?"

She told of giving birth to five children and seeing them sold into slavery, crying "with my mother's grief" when "none but Jesus heard me. . . . And ain't I a woman?"

The chairwoman of that convention was to write later: "She had taken us up in her strong arms, turning the whole tide in our favor."

Who would've guessed that this wise and famous freedom fighter was that little girl, born between chores in a basement of a forgotten inn nobody even knows for sure when?

Somewhere, in some forgotten and unnoticed corner of the world, just as we read these words, there are other babies being born in hospitals, in alleys, in ghettos, and refugee camps, who are destined by circumstance and calling, by determination and courage, to be sojourners of truth; to dream dreams and to see visions. To change history.

We must listen out for them.

SCOTT

—◯

August 4, 1979, was mostly sunny in Charlotte,
North Carolina. *The Muppet Movie* was drawing
crowds at the neighborhood theater. Shopping cen-
ters had specials on back-to-school jeans; and a
hometown, piano-playing cat named Pumpkin went
into the finals at the All-American Glamour Kitty
Contest in Florida.

But for Anne and Dan, the day was not sunny.

Even all these years later, they have to struggle to
concentrate on life's lighter side: the shopping trips,
the family movies. When the doorbell rang early that
Saturday morning, these parents woke up to a nightmare.

"It was almost three in the morning," Dan explained. "I saw two highway patrolmen standing on our front steps. Our next-door neighbor was with them. I looked at their faces. They didn't have to say a word. We knew."

What they knew in that split second of instinctive reaction—but what now seems heartbreakingly unreal—is that their teenage son, Scott, had been killed in an automobile accident. A drunk driver had run a light.

On an interstate out on the edge of town at 12:55 A.M., Anne and Dan joined the ranks of bereaved parents, an emotionally isolated and devastated army of mothers and fathers who must struggle with grief of the deepest sort. Often, this battle becomes a way of life and results in the breakdown of marriages, loss of communication with surviving children, and a frantic dependence on alcohol and drugs to ease the pain and guilt. Sometimes, emotions are even boarded up behind religious platitudes.

Dan remembers the trip to the morgue that night, waiting half an hour outside the adjoining jail with a roomful of derelicts. And finally identifying the body of his dead son.

"I came home and just held Anne. We didn't say anything. What was there to say? How can you communicate? Even with the people you love the most, grief has a way of ending all sentences, numbing all thoughts—paralyzing people."

They soon discovered another dimension of grief: Grief isolates. A gap exists, even in the well-intended outpourings of sympathy from friends. The church, by sheer facts of numbers, cannot provide the long-term, around-the-clock nurture of all those who mourn. But what Anne and Dan were most amazed to discover was that our socially sanctioned, "normal" ritualized means of expressing grief is nonexpression. There shalt be no breast-beating, no fear, no rage. There is a subtle taboo against crying, screaming, touching, holding, giving way.

"This is especially true for men," Dan said. "I really expected to pull myself out of it; to deal privately with it; to keep it to myself."

But the life-draining force of their suffering did not get cleared away with the neighbors' empty casserole dishes. Dan went back to work, and the days demanded their normal routine.

Then life began to curdle.

"I thought I was going crazy," Anne said softly.

Eventually, they joined a support group for bereaved parents. They talked with a woman whose husband had said he refused to grieve, that he had cried when his mother died, and that he never planned to cry again. Even when his only child was killed.

They found out they weren't the only ones who had church people tell them they were being punished for their sins and the only way to find peace was to repent.

That, Anne remembered, had been her lowest moment.

She says that sometimes it is people who are not involved with you emotionally who can help the most. "I think we made our friends nervous and uncomfortable. Nobody knows what to say. Grief is embarrassing, you know."

"If there are any cracks in the marriage," Dan added, "and I don't guess any marriage is perfect, then grief seems to make the cracks bigger. It's awful to see someone you love hurt when you know you can't help and you hurt, too."

Anne said, "There were times when I really thought I was losing my mind. Scott's death . . . our daily life . . . the sun coming up and going down . . . everything seemed unreal. People who have not experienced it just don't know."

Statistics document that the death of a child is life's most devastating experience and the best predictor of mental and physical illness in a person's adult life. Studies also show that 50 to 80 percent of couples who have experienced the death of a child are now divorced or separated.

Anne and Dan will never "get over" Scott's death.

Anne says that cooking a pot of spaghetti—Scott's favorite—is a major undertaking. Dan notices every teenage boy in a crowd, especially when they are laughing.

"If you know someone who faces the loss of a child," Anne said, "don't worry about saying the wrong thing; just be there. Try to get them in a support group. Above all, for heaven's sake, don't tell them it's God's will that their child died. That's an insult to everyone. Especially God."

TONYA LYNN

I am sitting in the neighborhood branch library while our sixth grader picks out books for her science project. Ever since I refused to pay her overdue charges for her, she has refused to let me decide which books she can check out. It's more democratic this way, but it takes about half an hour longer.

All of a sudden, I hear a crunching noise. Like termites chewing into a microphone. Next to me is a skinny little girl about four or five, nursing a giant bag of M&M's. She reads my mind.

"You want some M&M's, don'tcha? My name is Tonya Lynn and my mama says to sit here and not bother anybody while she looks up something in the cyclopedius."

"Thanks," I say "but I don't care for any," which is, of course, a big lie, because what I really would like is to snatch that whole bag from her and wolf it down without a thought about flab and cholesterol.

She chews on. With her mouth open. The noise is driving me wild.

"Read any good books lately?" I ask. Maybe she has been taught not to talk and eat at the same time.

"Nope," she says. "I don't know how to read."

Another fistful of candy goes into her mouth.

"Won't it be fun to learn?" I say in my nice-mother voice.

"Nope," she says after swallowing big. "I like for other people to read to me. See, whenever I ask a question, my mother just, pow! tells me the answer. Whenever my older brother asks a question, my mother says, 'Go look it up.' "

She grins at me, making her point. It's a big, juicy, sweet, brown-green-yellow-red grin. "Wanna play a game?" she asks.

"Sure," I say.

"OK. I'll ask you a question, and if you get the right answer, I'll give you an M&M. You gotta play fair, though, because I might not know the answer and you might try to lie, and that would be cheating. OK?"

"OK."

"Ummmm . . . What is the name of this country we're in?"

"The United States of America."

"Right! You want yellow or green?"

"Yellow." I decided to turn my winnings over to my daughter—if I didn't die of old age before she is ready to leave.

"Who discovered it?"

"Christopher Columbus."

"Right! Who made up the world?"

"God."

"Right! Who made up light bulbs?"

"Thomas Edison."

"Promise?"

"Well, with a little help from Benjamin Franklin."

By the time my daughter is stamped and checked out, I have twelve M&M's out of about twenty-five questions. I missed the ones on who lives next door to her, how old her dog is, and how many worms there are in the whole world.

"Here comes your last question," she says as we get up to leave. "How come people are different colors? How come they come in all different flavors, like you and me?"

Silence. It's like that TV commercial, "When E. F. Hutton speaks . . ." Two people look up from their magazines. A man in the reference section lowers his glasses and turns around. My daughter's jaw clenches on her twelve M&M's.

"Uh," I say, "the sun, I think, over the years made people in different places around the world . . . uh . . . made their skin different colors."

"Wrong."

"Well, I think it was planned that way, to make things more interesting."

"Wrong."

"I mean . . . genes, that's it. The genes tell each other what color to make us, depending on—"

"Wrong."

"I give up."

She dumps out the last two pieces of candy, balls up the empty bag, and stuffs it into her pocket.

"Well, see," she says, "God was out painting the sky one day, and He was using red, yellow, orange, brown, and green."

"What happened to blue?" asks my daughter.

"It was sunset. You don't need blue when you paint sunsets. Anyway, see, God was out painting sunsets and He was using these M&M colors, and suddenly, way off in the distance there was this huge, big clash of thunder. *Boom! Cra-a-a-sh!*"

All around the library, people look over in amazement as she goes through a whole repertoire of storm noises, but she doesn't seem to notice.

"It scared God so bad, He spilled the paint, and it

fell all over the world and all over people down below."

We all chew and think about this. I don't know why I have to ask this next question. I was sure she'd have an answer. "What about white?"

"Simple," she said. "You white people didn't get any of God's paint on you, because you must've been too busy doing other stuff to be out watching Him paint the sky."

"Well," says my daughter, coming to my rescue. "There are green M&M's, but no green people."

"Yes, there are so," she says. "On Mars."

On the way home, I think about how I wish I were as wise, as full of confidence as my new friend. And as skinny.

Before we get home, my skin has a slight tinge of green to it.

ANNE

Her real name was Annelies Marie, but people called her Anne. Except her mother. Sometimes, when her mother was feeling especially impatient or sentimental, she called Anne by her real name.

Like most teenagers of any name or place, Anne was in love with life—one minute, humming and giggling, then when somebody looked at her wrong or a dark thought came out from the corners of her mind, she would fight tears and bite her lip. She wondered what it would be like to be in love, and took up almost a whole page in her diary when she got her first kiss. She wasn't precocious or brilliant. Her grades in school were average, at best. She was not beautiful—but she had spirit and spunk and could smile on the outside, and while those things did not save her life, they made her immortal.

Anne Frank.

It's odd, isn't it, that one of the best-sellers of all times was not written by a "writer" or a great "teacher" or a world leader. It was written by a teenage girl hiding in an attic.

Anne had two birthdays in that attic. She was barely thirteen the summer afternoon in 1942 when her family gathered up a few things and walked in the pouring rain across Amsterdam to a warehouse above her father's grocery business. On August 1, 1944—two months after her fifteenth birthday—Nazi police burst through the door. Yanking open drawers, ripping mattresses, the police stuffed jewelry in their pockets and looked for hidden money. Then, shoving Anne and her family down the steps, into waiting cars, they drove off. No one immediately noticed the red-checkered diary left behind.

Anne was sixteen when she came down with typhus in Bergen-Belsen. Her mother would die of exhaustion, her sister of malnutrition. Only her father would be found alive, liberated by Russians at Auschwitz. Anne never knew all this. She died three months before her seventeenth birthday.

Nor did she have any idea that years later, over two thousand young people would march in the rain to Bergen-Belsen to place flowers on the mass grave into which she had been thrown like a piece of garbage.

"[No one] will be interested in the unbosoming of a thirteen-year-old schoolgirl," she writes in the first pages of her diary. She was wrong. That diary is translated into over thirty languages, her name a household word. The attic on the Prinsengracht Canal in Amsterdam is now a museum.

A week after the Franks' arrest, a family friend found the diary and, after the war, gave it to Anne's father. In 1937, though turned down by two Dutch publishing houses, it came out under the title *Diary of a Young Girl*. Ever since, people have turned to that attic prison where the only sunlight came from the unquenchable spirit of a teenage girl whom teachers had found average. Through this dreamy adolescent, we watch the world grow dark, fear moving through every aspect of life like a cancer on the loose.

We know from the outset how it will all end, but Anne sees things differently. Even as the news sputtering in over the radio grows worse and worse. Anne continues to write happy stories about elves, bears, and an old dwarf. Even as she sits crammed up in the secret corner of a world gone mad, she talks about playing Ping-Pong and how good the sun feels on her face. Even after she loses one of her many private bouts with the encroaching loneliness, she says in her heart she knows people are basically kind, and that no matter what happens, good will win out.

Did it? Will it again?

A hundred years before Anne Frank wrote in her diary, an old British scholar, sitting in his soft leather chair and enjoying a good cigar, wrote these immortal words: "The pen is mightier than the sword." It was a teenage girl who not only proved it, but went one better:

In the long run, the sharpest weapon of all is a kind and gentle spirit.

MAC

—9

Maybe in the long run, love never faileth—but it sure can backfireth. All of us have memories of a painful Valentine massacre somewhere along the line.

The first time my heart made its maiden voyage into the world of True Love, it got smashed to pieces.

May-September romances seldom work out, but I didn't know that then. He was in the twelfth grade. I was in the seventh. It was the year they tore down the old junior high school to build a new one, and grades seven through twelve crowded into one school on two shifts.

I thanked my lucky stars that he and I ended up

on the same shift. Later, if I could've gotten my hands on Cupid, I would have stuck him in the backside with his sharpest arrow.

Because, by the second day of school, I was in love.

His locker was across the hall from mine. He had very white teeth and a Johnny Ray hairdo. His name was Mac.

After months of staring at him through the slits in my locker door, I finally lost my mind. Maybe I ate too many cinnamon red hots or spent too much time listening to the *Hit Parade*—but that Valentine's Day, I skipped required assembly and left a love letter in Mac's locker.

The only smart thing I did was to sign it "Tiffany."

Tiffany was just one of hundreds of names I wished my parents has used instead of *Ina*. To me, it sounded like the name of a beautiful princess. This was years before Barbie dolls and soap opera names became popular, and there were no Tiffanys in the whole school. I checked.

In those days, people were named after relatives, and as far as I knew, nobody else in the whole world had any relatives named Ina. Whatever possessed my parents to give me such a name? It sounded like the name of somebody's pet iguana.

This was the first love letter I ever wrote to anybody. All I had to go on was listening to Pat Boone croon about writing "Love Letters in the Sand," and somebody else equally as sappy singing, "P.S., I Love You." I did not have beginner's luck.

I told him he was wonderful, which turned out to be a big lie.

Then I really unzipped my heart.

Mac had a certain look about him. His eyes stayed at half mast most of the time. Bedroom eyes, someone at the pajama parties had called them. It drove us seventh-graders crazy.

It is really hard for me to believe I was ever so stupid, but this is—as I told you—a story of *True* love, emphasis on the *true* and not "love." Mac's eyes were not his fault.

In my letter, I told Mac that a friend of a friend had told me about how he'd lost one of his eyes in that awful car wreck (this was the story making the rounds at the seventh-grade girls' lunch table), that I knew about his *glass eye,* but I thought it looked real even though sometimes it watered and turned red when he got tired, but that certainly didn't matter to me.

Back then, not only was my brain small, so was my body. I could stand inside my locker and close the door on myself—which is what I did after assembly when Mac returned to his locker to read my letter.

I watched him as—jacket slung over one shoulder, books balanced on his hips—he ripped open the envelope with his white, white teeth.

In my dreams, he would read and reread it slowly, savoring every word and noticing the neat way the *i*'s were dotted with little circles. Then he would put it carefully in the pocket closest to his heart. That's what I would have done if someone had written me a letter like that.

On second thought, I'd have probably had an aneurysm.

If you had been standing in that locker with me, you could have heard my heart snap in two when Mac let out that first shout of laughter. He waved my precious secret in the air and, killing me softly with every whoop and holler, asked if everybody wanted to see something hard to believe.

All that day, his friends called him Cyclops.

Turns out he didn't have a glass eye after all. Just hay fever.

I spent the rest of that day in my locker, blowing my nose on my gym shorts. As soon as I got home, I worked up a cough that by suppertime had my mother worried I might be coming down with something. My temperature turned out to be 103, thanks to the old run-the-thermometer-under-warm-water trick.

Anything to get out of school for the rest of my life.

All that winter and spring, Cyclops (the name stuck) walked the halls with his arms around this girl or that from a harem of cheerleaders, student-government presidents, and May Court queens. I lived in horror that one day he would have a vision and learn that Tiffany was really the girl who jumped inside her locker every time he rounded the corner.

The gods were with me on that score. He never knew. My luck got better, and soon I even forgot, but not without learning something: Love not only can warm the cockles of the heart . . . it can burn holes in it.

Whoever decided it was better to have loved and lost than not to have loved at all never fell for an older man with hay fever.

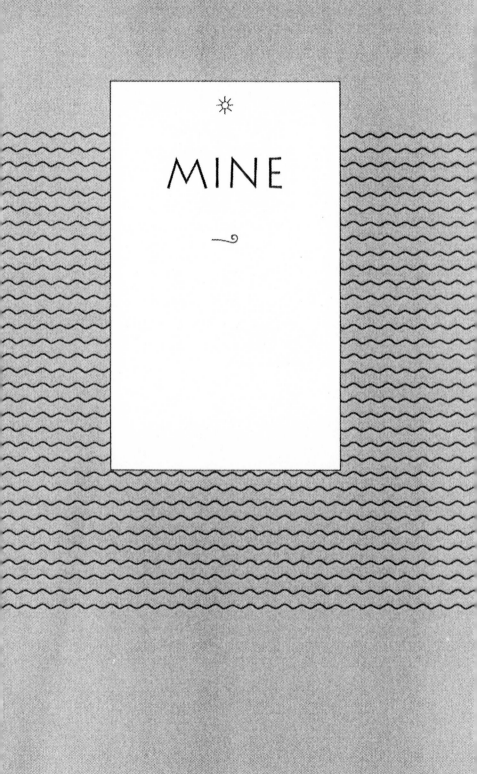

MINE

I t is no coincidence that every great teacher of every world religion uses stories to teach the truth. You can show me a doctrine, preach me a sermon, recite me a creed—but tell me a story, and I will remember.

It works that way in families, too. The only way we can share ourselves with one another, to pass on our beliefs and our spirit, is to tell the stories of our life. In good oral tradition, it used to be that Grandmother or Aunt Faye or Cousin Jake—not Hollywood or some way-off television writer—came up with the situation comedies, the dramas, the mysteries that kept us spellbound after supper on the porch or around the kitchen table before bed.

Best of all, the characters in those stories were not actors playing a part, following someone else's script. They were the real people living in us, and through us, and with us, every day, in both ordinary and extraordinary ways.

If we are not careful, we will become a family, a community, and eventually a culture, raised on other people's stories. If that happens, we will become strangers to one another. And to ourselves. "Once upon a time" is the most exciting phrase in any language, and when what follows comes from inside our own hearts and mind's eye— we give a gift that cannot be measured in time or dollars.

Here are some of my stories, told in hopes that you can find some of your own in them. Then it will be your turn.

MAKING BELIEVE
THE TRUTH

⟿

She was my best friend. So smart, so much fun to be with. But sometimes, friends grow apart over the years, especially in friendships like ours.

Her name was Verifrickus. I don't know where such a name came from. I don't remember when she started coming to see me. I do, however, remember when she stopped.

We were driving home from a visit to my grandmother's, and I was lying across the backseat of the car with my feet sticking up on the window ledge, watching the world fly by.

It suddenly seemed a little babyish for a six-year-old to have a friend nobody else could see or hear. Or believe in.

So Verifrickus disappeared right then and there, just like the trees that flew out of sight past the car windows, like dancers making a quick, silent exit.

But I'll never forget her.

She used to sit at the dinner table and fish the cooked carrots off my plate, drop them into her napkin, then ask to be excused so she could flush them down the toilet.

She knew exactly where my brother's shins were under the table, and her aim was perfect.

Once, she actually told my father to shut up. She said it very quietly, but he still heard. She never, never did that again.

Through thick and thin Verifrickus was there. I think about the night my little sister took a sip of some ammonia that had been carelessly stored in a 7UP bottle. Her lips swelled, she screamed bloody murder, and the doctor rushed over.

Verifrickus came and watched the whole thing with me from my hiding place on the back steps. The whole thing was my fault, I told my only friend. But God should know that just because you'd wished your baby sister would drop dead didn't mean you actually wanted her to die.

By far, the most fun Verifrickus and I had together was when we would take my collection of little glass animals out in the garden in back of my house. We'd build villages for them out of sticks and acorns. If we were lucky, we sometimes found mushrooms that became a home for a ceramic squirrel or an umbrella for the frog with the chipped-off leg.

Verifrickus understood me, but people did not understand her. Chuck Lambeth once caught me and Verifrickus playing make-believe, and he went off telling everyone he'd seen me talking to myself. If anybody had ever asked me why I wanted to go to heaven, I'd tell them it was because I knew Chuck Lambeth would not be there.

Once—just once—I tried to tell one of my friends about how important Verifrickus was and how I didn't care if she was real or not, because it was fun to pretend.

The friend listened and acted as if she didn't think it was anything too awful, my confession. Later, I saw her standing by the water fountain telling what I said to a group of other kids. They were laughing.

It was a confusing lesson. Real friends are supposed to stick by you.

In all of the bad things Verifrickus did—kicking my brother, sassing my father, even wetting the bed once—she never laughed at me.

Verifrickus never came back after that car trip home, when I watched the trees slip off into the night. But years later, I met some of her relatives.

One was named Ashley, and she lived in the closet behind the clothes in my own three-year-old-daughter's room. Another didn't really have a name, but he used to eat butter out of my refrigerator and let Popsicles melt on the sofa.

They, too, eventually flew off somewhere along the trip out of childhood, but I am sure that sometimes they are remembered—and thanked—for sticking by their special friend.

Sometimes the best magic of all is found inside your own head.

CHILDHOOD
EPIPHANIES

—9

One of the memories I have as a child is of lying on the floor under our Christmas tree and looking up through its branches at the star on top. I'd never quite understood, and certainly never seen with my own eyes, the kind of star that shone in the Bible stories. To be so bright, so crystal clear, it beamed all the way to the other side of the world, yet focused directly over Bethlehem and flashed a path to the exact spot where anybody who just paid attention could find Jesus if they wanted to—it was a thought too big to fit in my head all at once.

But there under the tree, looking up through those branches dripping with tinsel, colored bubble lights casting their rainbow magic up to the top of the tree and dancing on the ceiling, I could believe anything was possible.

Later on in my search for explanations, I read scientific theories from astronomers who explained the Christmas night sky with statistics and timetables, saying it was Halley's comet or a meteor or shower or a hovering of vapors. I debated odds and possibilities, testimonials and assertions, but none have been more inspiring, or done a better job of convincing me, than my under-the-tree epiphany in the living room of my house there on Providence Road some two thousand years later.

I have looked at a lot of Christmas trees and into half a century's worth of evening skies since then, and even though I have never seen a star any more convincing than the ones in my childhood living room, sometimes, when I'm driving home from work and see the sunset pasted up against the windows of my car, its beauty catches in my throat, and I get those same feelings I had as I watched the bubble lights and dancing shadows at Christmas all those years ago.

Whoever is painting those stars of memory, and now these sunsets and night skies, has something up a sleeve. It's a talent no artist, no middle-aged woman, no kid with a runaway imagination who spends hours lying among the presents and looking at a lit-up star, could possibly put into words.

Good art never can be explained, be it sacred or secular.

It never matches the sofa.

People who buy a painting because it color-coordinates with the drapes aren't really listening with their eyes. Art, says John Ruskin, is one soul talking with another.

Coming home from work in a gray haze of exhaust fumes and ozone, dreary world news and traffic reports coming over the radio like sad six o'clock sermons—if the night-sky artist had wanted to "match the sofa," he'd have chosen something Gothic or surrealistic: a Dali or a Jackson Pollock. He'd have spread his palette with dabs of ashtray gray and Weejun-loafer brown.

Instead, the sky up over the dark woods and gray river road reminds me of lessons from childhood and my under-the-tree paintings there in my parents' house: bubble lights and reds of every shade and shimmer transforming an ordinary living-room world into one full of light and promise.

PLAYING IT
BY EAR

—૭

If I didn't know better, I'd have sworn "Dear Abby" was talking about my Uncle Hervey.

Tennessee made the headlines in Abby's column when a woman wrote about her husband's family and their tendency to crush ribs and deflate lungs when they hugged people hello.

The last time she went to visit, the woman told Abby, her mother-in-law hugged her with such enthusiasm, it sprained her neck. Her husband once gave one of his Tennessee cousins such a hearty greeting, he broke three of the poor guy's ribs.

Sounds like some of my kinfolk. My Uncle

Hervey had a way of saying hello that made you see stars. His specialty wasn't ribs. It was ears.

"Say hello to your Uncle Hervey!"

The first time I heard those words, I innocently padded over, looked up into the stratosphere (he was at least twelve feet tall) and did what I was told.

"Hello, Uncle Herv-*ouch!*"

He didn't just tug or pinch ears. He grabbed hold and twisted. Sometimes, the lobe would end up on top when he finally let go, which he did only after he'd gone into painful detail in his deep scratchy voice about how he remembered when my daddy was my age and how I'd inherited his squinty-eyed smile.

We always knew which cousins had just come from saying hello to Uncle Hervey. They were very quiet, too busy swallowing baby tears to say anything—and they held their head funny, like they were trying to keep something from falling off.

But the ear twistings were a small price to pay for having an Uncle Hervey who owned the local railroad company and every visit would arrange for us to ride from Laurinburg to Hamlet, up with the engineer who let us blow the whistle every time we came to a crossing.

One summer at the beach, when we knew Uncle Hervey was coming, my brother Jimmy went down to the pier and bought out the supply of Bazooka bubble gum in the little Tootsie-Roll-style packs they used to come in, five wads for a nickel.

For days, we chewed and chewed until we got the sugar out and could work with the gum to design and mold a fake set of ears to fit our faces. It took lots of gum to come up with two that looked real. And matched.

The night Uncle Hervey was due, we went Rock-Paper-Scissors to determine who would go first when time came to "say hello to Uncle Hervey."

We figured that once he actually did what he'd been trying all these years to do—namely, unscrew an ear from some child's head—maybe he would be satisfied. Or at least get the hint. One twist, and he'd have a pink, flesh ear stuck to his fingers.

I suggested we really get even by having ketchup in our hand so when we grabbed the side of our head after the first twist, we'd send blood gushing out, and Uncle Hervey would *really* be sorry.

But my brother Bobby didn't think that was such a good idea. Especially since he was the Rock to three Papers and no Scissors.

Bobby went in, Uncle Hervey twisted, the Bazooka ear fell off, everybody laughed, and Bobby came out.

When my turn came to "go say hello to Uncle Hervey," fate was not so kind. Before I'd taken two steps, my left Bazooka fell off. Uncle Hervey took one look at me, smiled his squinty-eyed smile, grabbed my naked left ear by the stem, and wound it like a pocket watch.

As time passed and we got older, Uncle Hervey lost interest in our ears and took to knocking the wind out of my brothers with slaps on the back. We girls got something between a charley horse and a slug on the shoulder. Eventually, Uncle Hervey became too weak to slap or hug or even speak, and going in to say hello was something we dreaded, not because of a tug on the ear, but because of a tug on the heart.

My legacy from him after all these years is a squinty-eyed smile that's been recycled in varying degrees in my own three children; a stop-dead-in-your-tracks love of train whistles; and a left ear that is definitely larger than the right.

SASHAYING
WITH THE
LAW

—◡

Once, when I must have looked terribly old and wrinkled, my children asked me if back in the olden days when I was a little girl, there had been such things as Saturdays.

Was there ever. Big, fat, delicious Saturdays spent exploring every square inch of my territory, which ran from our house on Providence Road, down past the Town House Restaurant, Reid's Supermarket, Park Place Pharmacy, then to the outer boundaries of Al Browne's Service Station—a good half-hour away by bike.

Providence Road looked very different then. There was a miniature golf course where Wachovia

Bank is now, a clump of woods instead of Myers Park Shopping Center. The Woman's Exchange was the only gift shop I can remember anywhere on Providence Road. It sold cross-stitched pillowcases, and the saleslady handed out lemon drops. People came in to shop, and if they had money, they paid. If they didn't, they said they would when they did have some. The Woman's Exchange is long gone now, and there are fancy new shops of all kinds up and down that old familiar trail. They all have their bad-check policies, their shoplifting warnings, and their triple-locking doors.

One of those new specialty shops is in the old Gourmajenko house, a huge pink monstrosity that straddles four sides of a whole block. I haven't been inside, but from the outside, it looks just like it did on the Saturdays of my childhood.

The Fearless Foursome, we called ourselves. Bobby and Dickie, twins from across the street who had nerves of steel and no particular time they had to be home; Sally, my red-headed, joined-at-the-hip best friend; and me, who thought it a matter of personal honor to punch out anybody who called me either a chicken, "Freckle Face," or the preacher's kid. Mainly because I was all three.

One Saturday morning, we'd gone by the golf course and played marble golf. (No clubs or money needed, just a couple of marbles, a small course, and a friendly owner.) Then we'd checked the crates of discarded soft drinks. If there was an inch or two of Orange Crush or root beer left in any of them, we'd gulp it down and count ourselves lucky. My mother never knew, and I never did catch a single one of those awful diseases she would have worried about had she known—unless you call stupidity a disease, which is something I definitely had a bad case of the Saturday I messed with the Gourmajenkos.

We'd gotten bored with the golf game, so wandered down Providence Road, washed a few windshields at the Esso station, ran from a gang of my brother's friends we caught smoking behind the Manor Theatre. We ended up hanging over the stucco wall surrounding the Gourmajenko house.

"Wonder what it's like inside."

"Bet a spy lives there. It's not an American name, you know. My dad says it's Russian."

"What if it's an old, old man who has gone crazy and at night goes out and gets people and cuts them up in little pieces and hides them in suitcases down in the basement . . . after he drinks their blood."

"Shoot, that doesn't scare me."

"Me, neither."

Silence.

"Bet I know which one of us *is* a chicken."

They knew, and I knew. And they knew I knew they knew.

"Scaredy-cat . . . yellow-britches."

"Look, she's so scared, her freckles are turning yellow."

"Nah. She's not scared. She's just a goody-goody."

That's when I got stupid. I flung myself over the wall, ran across the driveway, climbed a window casing, held onto the gutter, and pulled myself up on the wrought-iron balcony overlooking the courtyard. My legs stung from crawling through the prickly bushes, and a place on the gutter had jabbed into my shoulder. I wanted to look to see if it was bleeding, but mostly, I was so scared, I would've counted myself lucky if God Himself had stepped out on that balcony and taken me up in glory.

But there are stronger juices than fear. Pride, for one. And I wasn't about to let such a sweet moment pass without being a show-off. So I dropped my jeans and did a little hula dance for the benefit of my three friends. They waved, gave out a chorus of Saturday-morning laughing fits, the kind that give you hiccups.

Suddenly, they got this awful look on their faces, yelled *"Look behind you!"* and dove for cover.

Behind me in the French doorway of that second-floor balcony, approximately three feet from my sashaying behind, was not God Almighty and not a German *or* Russian spy, but an old lady in a long white nightgown. All I remember about her was seeing the whites of her eyes and that little thing hanging down in back of her throat as she tried to scream.

The police came and picked me up.

"What's your name, little girl?"

Silence.

And more silence. I was not going to tell them my name or my address or phone number or the names of my friends who ran away or what I was doing on the balcony of Mrs. Gourmajenko's house. I was not particularly proud of the fact that I came from a long line of Presbyterian ministers, but I was not about to add criminal, trespasser, or tattletale to the family ranks. They could hang me, shoot me, imprison me for the rest of my life, but I would not tell them my name. I never did.

And they didn't shoot me, either. It might have been easier if they had, because they made me promise I would tell my parents what I had done. Confessing to a priest behind a curtain in a dark cathedral may be good for the soul, but telling my father I had been caught breaking and entering the Gourmajenko house, then mooned an old lady on her own balcony—well, it caused me great pains in certain areas, and the Fearless Foursome was short one player for several Saturdays after that.

Both my father and the police made me promise I would never, never, go near that old house again.

That was forty years ago, and now they've made a shopping villa, a restaurant, and who knows what else out of the old Gourmajenko mansion. The balcony is still there. The window. The wall. It's supposed to really be nice.

Great place for a Saturday visit.

But I have promises to keep.

PRAYING
OVER PRUNES

—๑

One Thanksgiving, many years ago, I got in a big argument with God and ended up being sent to my room. The family had all gathered together, and when time came to ask the Lord's blessing, asking Him, as the old table grace goes, to "make us truly thankful"—I flatly refused.

I'd spent all morning before that Great Feast arguing with the cooks in the kitchen, who insisted on trying a new recipe for turkey dressing. Dressing, by the way, was my favorite part of Thanksgiving. Maybe even then I was a budding vegetarian, because I paid only nibbling respect to the slab of white meat my father would serve up. I preferred the squash, another traditional dish, and always asked for seconds. Likewise with green beans and cranberry Jell-O. Ambrosia was a favorite until the day my brother told me the white stuff in it was sheep hair. If I'd asked my mother, she would have told me it was coconut, but I made the mistake of asking my older brother.

The same brother, by the way, who once switched my plain milk with my grandmother's buttermilk. I spent that meal up in my room, too, because I spit the first swallow all over the centerpiece—and the second, bull's-eye on my brother.

Anyway, of all the Thanksgiving blessings, dressing was my favorite. This particular Thanksgiving, someone had given my mother a recipe for dressing made with dried *prunes* in it. Prunes reminded me of something I saw in a jar at the doctor's office the time I wandered off while my little sister was being chased down for a tetanus booster.

No prune was going into my body.

I asked if a bowl of unpruned dressing could be made specially for me, but my mother was big on the try-it-you-might-like-it theory of feeding her young.

By dinner time, I'd worked myself into a snit.

Saying a blessing over prunes, pretending to be grateful, became a matter of personal honor. I would go to dinner, I would bow my head, but I would not pray. Although I wasn't exactly sure what a hypocrite was, I knew it had to do with telling lies, and I knew you went to hell for it. Furthermore, if my mother really loved me, she would have made me some unpruned dressing, so I decided I would not bless and I would not eat. I would starve. Then she'd be sorry.

The tradition in our family was to go around the table and have everyone thank God in person for what they were about to receive. Since I was not going to receive anything, I refused.

A hush fell over the family.

"Bless the food," my father said.

"No, sir, I will not," I said.

But that's not all I said. I felt inspired.

"If prunes are so wonderful, how come they need blessing? How come any of it needs blessing. Is it a poison?"

I got a little carried away with this newfound theology, raising my voice so not only everybody at the table could hear, but God Himself might sit up and take notice. Maybe learn a few pointers.

Well, the upshot of the thing is that I spent that Thanksgiving in my room.

As dessert was being passed around down in the dining room, the sky outside suddenly grew dark, and a storm moved in. Rain hit the windows like tiny darts. Trees struggled against the wind, and lightning sizzled so close by, I could feel hairs on my arms stand up and take notice. I was convinced the thunder was taking my ears off their hinges.

I'd already had enough time to think about things and was pretty sure I'd messed up down there at the dinner table, acting like a spoiled brat and sassing my father. The storm convinced me. It was God, sending His wrath upon me. A sure sign I should repent.

Which I did.

THE TRUTH
ABOUT SANTA

—☉

The day school let out for the Christmas vacation that year, I faced a major turning point in my life. I was in the second grade, and a big-shot third grader took me on top of the jungle gym and solemnly announced that there was no Santa Claus.

Never had been and never would be.

All the fat, jolly men who sat around in stores handing out candy canes and getting their pictures taken were fakes. Now, how did I like that, my friend asked.

To tell the truth, it was a real shock. I had bought the whole package: snow-covered chalets in the North Pole; that certain cotton-candy smile; that deep, know-it-all laugh; reindeer with Eastern Air-line noses. All those lists I had made! All the chocolate milk and cookies set out!

Who read my notes? Who ate those snacks? Where did all the toys come from?

I had a lot to think about.

My snitch spared none of the gory details. The toys were ordered from Sears, not made by tiny elves. They didn't come from the North Pole. They came from the attic, and that noise I heard last Christmas Eve, which I thought had been Santa, was probably my daddy slamming the garage door where my new bike had been hidden behind the picnic table.

Come to think of it, it was pretty ridiculous to believe somebody could actually dash across rooftops and squeeze down every chimney in the whole world in one single night.

But the biggest insult to my intelligence was all that nonsense about not shouting or pouting, and how Santa was some all-knowing moral spy who knew when you were sleeping, and hung around invisible all season, just waiting for some little kid to mess up and get blitzed from the list.

Blackmail. That's what it was. Parental blackmail.

That Christmas Eve, my contribution to Santa's snack was licorice. I watched with utter amazement as my older brothers and sister hung their stockings.

How could they be so dumb? I hid mine behind the piano bench.

You can bet I hadn't made any list, or lined up with any of those ignoramuses in the department stores to have a picture taken with some strange old man with a pillow in his pants. None of that phony stuff ever again.

The tradition in our family on Christmas morning was to line up on the stairs according to age. That was my last year on the bottom step as the baby of the family. In more ways than one. By Easter, I had a new sister.

My mother and daddy loaded the camera, turned on the tree lights, and called out as they had done and would do for many Christmases to come, "Nothing down here but cornbread and switches! . . ."

For a moment, I had the sinking feeling they were exactly right in my case. I had made no list, seen no visions of sugarplums, and certainly hadn't been good for goodness' sake. It was with fear and trembling that I walked into the living room.

I can still see the room exactly as it was. There on the floor by the chimney was a real nurse's kit. It had real hospital trays, syringes, scissors, tweezers, a stethoscope, medicine bottles with sugar pills—all neatly arranged around a black bag with my name on it.

If I had pored over a list for two solid weeks, I

couldn't have come up with anything so perfect. For months, I had diagnosed and tended all the make-believe epidemics and illnesses, the imagined catastrophes that befell my dolls and stuffed animals. I'd even talked our dog Brownie into playing half-dead so I could cure him—but I had no idea how much I wanted a real nurse's kit. In my wildest dreams, I had never imagined anything that was as wonderful as the gift I got that Christmas.

Even though I had been taken in by all that Santa Claus stuff, I wasn't so dumb that I couldn't figure out a few things all by myself. How could any guy way up in the North Pole know how much I would like a nurse's kit? If he had known, probably he would have brought one of those play kind with all the plastic junk. This was the real thing.

I'll never forget that Christmas. When I saw the nurse's kit, I began to think about what it means to be loved. I began to see how Santa Claus is a fairy tale that comes alive when we are old enough to understand the real magic of a parent's love, and how that love is more exciting, more wonderful, than any red-suited man who visits only once a year and needs a list to know what we want.

Some people are brought to the manger by a star. For me, it was a nurse's kit.

THE FINAL VERSE

—♋

One Christmas—I guess I was about eight or nine—my father took me with him on a visit to a nursing home. As a Presbyterian minister, he would often, as he put it, "pay a call" on shut-ins in the congregation.

Lots of times, he took one of us along, especially around Christmas. Usually, when he went to the critical-care unit of a nursing home, we waited in the car; but, for some reason, this particular Christmas, I tagged along.

As we opened the heavy swinging doors that separated the sick from the well, I entered a world unlike anything I had known, and I was more frightened than I remember ever being before and maybe even since.

Going to visit older people had always been something I looked forward to. I got *oooed* and *ahhed* over, and, when talk shifted from me to something else, I most times had a candy cane to lick or a Whitman Sampler to keep me busy.

I liked the way my father had of making people laugh, and I felt important belonging to him. But this was different. These people did not look like people at all. They looked like bodies left behind after the people who lived in them had gone somewhere. I did not understand or want any part of what I saw and felt.

My father went to each bed, speaking gently to the patients, most of whom said nothing but lay like grown-up rag dolls in the half darkness.

There were pictures on the dresser: a lady in a pretty hat laughing at a baby on her hip; a kind-looking man in a business suit almost winking into the camera. I knew what name tags were. These must have been face tags, reminding nurses and doctors and strangers like me that these lost, forgotten people were once real.

Several wept silently. Most slept. A few looked at me and said nothing. Others looked through me, saying things I could not understand. One man thought my daddy was his daddy, and, coming alive at the recognition, called out in a little-boy voice that did not match his face, "Please, take me home."

A group of Christmas carolers came through the hall, and, as they got closer, I recognized what they were singing. It was "Joy to the World."

How cruel, I thought.

How inappropriate.

Just then, I head a voice from across the hall call out, "Little girl? Little girl? Come here."

I'd have never budged, except that my father took me by the shoulder and led the way.

"How old are you?" the voice wanted to know.

I couldn't remember.

"Would you sing that song to me?"

I wouldn't have if my father hadn't gotten me started: "And hea-ven and hea-ven and na-ture sing."

"Do you know the last verse?" the voice said.

"No, ma'am," I whispered.

"Promise me something, my dear," she said. "Learn it. It's the best verse of all."

We rode home in silence, my father and I. When we pulled up in the driveway and he turned off the car engine, neither of us got out.

"Why?" I asked. "I don't understand how God can let these people be like that."

It was a perfect time for a sermon. I was hanging on for some passage of Scripture, some simple sentence to memorize that would answer all such questions forever and ever.

Instead, my father said, "I don't know."

He waited for that to sink in and then went on. "But she is right. The last verse of 'Joy to the World' promises us that even when we are not who we are, even when it looks like we have been left behind or when we feel alone in the world—we can depend on the mystery of God's love."

The older I get, the more I think about those words in the last verse and all the other "wonders of love" we discover in this life.

Both of those voices from that night have long since been silenced, but their words ring in my ears as I celebrate Christmas.

And wonder still.

A WRINKLE
IN TIME

—9

"Mama," she said, crawling up in my lap and taking my cheeks between her hands, "will I ever get wrinkles?"

So. My little secret was out. She'd seen them, too: those stitch-pleats and gathers I'd seen face-to-face in the mirror lately. One morning, I thought I saw a few.

Couldn't be. Not yet.

Next morning, I leaned over the sink and took a long look. I'd never thought about what a crow's foot actually looks like up close, but a whole squadron of them had begun their migratory trek across

my face: around my eyes, tiptoeing across my forehead, running out from the edges of my mouth.

Digging trenches from my nose to my chin.

Time not only leaves footprints in the sands of
time, it scribbles messages all over your face, and no
matter how hard you try, time doesn't write in dis-
appearing ink.

"Will my face ever have creases?" she asked again,
running her fingers over the lines in my face, partly
to see if they were real, partly to comfort me because
they were. I tried to smile at her question, which of
course just made more wrinkles for her to notice.
She looked worried.

"Well," I said as I cleared my throat and got ready
for a Discussion, "everybody gets older."

"Are you old?"

"I probably look old to somebody who's four, like
you. But then, you look old compared to a newborn
baby, and I don't look so old compared to, say,
somebody who is maybe eighty or ninety. It's all
relative."

"Relatives die," she said. "Katie in my class was
out a week and I heard Mrs. Garr tell someone it
was because of a relative death."

"I didn't mean that kind of relative. I meant that
how old a person seems depends on what you com-
pare the person to. Katie's grandmother is a different

kind of relative. She was kin to Katie, and was old and had been sick for a long time. Probably her family was glad she was not going to have to suffer anymore. It was time for her to die. Sometimes when death comes, it's more of a friend than an enemy. Sometimes people are even happy about it, even though they know they will miss that person."

"When will you die?"

"I don't know."

"But, the more wrinkles you have, the closer you are to dying, right?"

"I guess you're right, but I don't think about it that way. At least, I try not to think about it that way."

"Why don't you *do* something about your wrinkles?"

"I don't think there's really much a person can do."

"What causes them anyway? Do they come from stuff like chewing with your mouth open when you were a little girl? Or making faces at your friends? Maybe it's like you tell me not to cross my eyes 'cause they might get stuck. Maybe if people didn't make faces at each other, they wouldn't get wrinkles."

When a four-year-old gets onto something, there's no telling where she will take it. She was half serious, half joking.

We were both quiet for a while, then I said, "I guess the only way you could never have wrinkles is if you never smiled or laughed or cried or frowned or made silly faces or acted surprised. If all your life you just kept your face still and frozen like a stone statue, maybe you'd not get wrinkles."

"You mean like this . . ." and she tried to stare me down without moving a muscle, then hopped out of my lap and stiff-legged it into the bathroom, hiked herself up on the sink, and looked at herself in the mirror.

"Is this how your face does when you are dead?" she wanted to know. "A dead person has to hold perfectly still, right?"

"That's one way to look at it, I guess."

"Then getting wrinkles keeps you from dying," she said.

"Or leading a pretty boring life," I added.

She looked at herself a little longer, then an idea came to her. I saw it land in her eyes as she slid down from the sink and came back over to sit in my lap again.

"Well, Mama," she said, squeezing my mouth up, trying to imagine what I'm going to look like when I really do get up there with Katie's grandmother. "I guess you can't help it if you get old and wrinkled on the outside. I just hope you never get old and wrinkled on the inside."

The life expectancy of the American woman is 75.2 years. According to the statistics, I'd just hit the halfway mark, so it's about time somebody explained to me in words I can really understand the meaning of it all. I could've gone out and paid a lot of money for books and advice sessions, courses on this age-old problem of facing the wrinkles of time. But how could they improve on what I learned from my own live-in philosopher, giving me the once-over and speaking from the heart?

THE FISHY FACTS

I don't know when my son George learned the facts of life. You think at the time you'll never forget these things, but you do. I do remember a comment he made to a kindergarten teacher several weeks before his sister was born.

"Your mommy is going to have a baby!" she said in that silly seesaw voice grownups for some reason use with anyone who comes below our knees.

"Yes, ma'am," says George.

"Is it going to be a boy or a girl?"

"I think so," says George.

Poor thing, he probably worried that we'd been

holding out on him and there was some other possibility we hadn't explained.

Kids don't really ask a lot of questions about these things. They just sit there like lumps while parents sweat through the whole nine yards. Every once in a while, Mom or Dad stops for breath, looking at the child for some flicker of understanding, some question to spur them along. Nothing.

All the kid does is stare at his feet, trying not to look surprised or grossed out.

Their father and I split the difference when it came to The Talk. He took our son aside, and I broke the news to our two daughters. I never did learn exactly what went on during their conversation, my son's and his father's. It took place on a fishing trip, just the two of them. The subject came up naturally, according to reports, when they saw some cows or bulls or whatever in a field. The only thing our son George told me about that trip was that they ate beef jerky and jelly beans for breakfast.

His dad said George took the Birds and Bees like he does most things: very thoughtfully.

"Do you have any questions?" his dad asked.

"Yes, sir."

"Ask me anything, son."

"How come that man at the trout farm asked if we wanted our fish dressed?"

FLUTING
THE BILL

‿୭

There's no good reason to take music and art out of the school curriculum. If I had my way, they would be in there ahead of math and science. Why? These days we need to be especially careful we don't turn technology into a god; facts and figures have powerful muscles but no personality.

Even Albert Einstein would agree. Imagination. he once said, is more important than knowledge.

But there is another reason. Art builds character and teaches you to believe in miracles. Especially if you are the parents of a budding artist.

When our kids were coming along, all fourth graders in their school were required to try out an instrument to play in the fifth-grade band. One afternoon my daughter came home with a note from school asking us to talk it over and help her decide which instrument she wanted to try out. Her band career began that night as she flipped through the *World Book,* considering the options.

Drums?

Too boyish.

The violin?

Too hard.

Trumpet?

Too loud.

Just before bed, she decided on the flute.

"Flute" and "cute" rhymed, she said. Something I am sure Jean-Pierre Rampal never thought of, so I guess that makes her one up on him even before she blew her first note.

It was a big day when she and I came home with her rent-to-buy flute, her flute-carrying case, flute-music stand, flute-cleaning cloth and care-of-the-flute instruction book.

She was ready.

The night before her first band practice, she laid everything out on the bed, called the dog into the room, and closed the door. Slowly she raised the flute to her mouth and blew.

Nothing. Not a sound.

She turned it around and blew at the other end,

just in case. She punched all the little buttons and blew into *those* holes as well. Just in case. She shook it a couple of times to maybe unlock things inside or wake them up or whatever their problem was, then cleared her throat, licked her lips, and blew again.

Nothing.

Sitting there cross-legged on the floor, she stared at the flute for a while. Even talked to it a little bit. The dog came over, took a few sniffs, a few licks, and turned to look at her as if to say, "You got a lemon here, pal."

"Mom!" she yelled. "We've been ripped off."

She handed me the flute. I blew and squeezed my lips and hummed through my nose. Nothing. I have to admit the thought occurred to me that she was right. It was cute, but it was broken.

"A flute flaw," I teased. "Try to say that five times in a row."

But she was not ready to laugh about it at this point, and by the next night, doubt had turned to despair.

"It won't do anything," she cried. "When I blow, nothing comes out but slobber. I had to use the cleaning cloth to wipe off the girl sitting next to me. I hate band. I don't want to be a flootist or a fleetist or whatever you call the dumb thing anyway."

"Playing the flute doesn't just happen like that,"

I said, snapping my fingers and launching into the old anything-worthwhile-takes-time routine. "Why not give it one more try?"

So, taking the dog with her, she went into her room and closed the door while I looked up at the ceiling and prayed for a miracle. I knew heaven was awfully busy with more important matters, but parents have no shame.

It turns out heaven is, as a matter of fact, very music-minded. Pretty soon, I was hearing things. The flute fluted.

"*Pffjlluuugghhh . . . Pffjlluuugghhh . . .*"

All night. All the next day. And the day after.

Pretty soon, I was on my knees again, praying for another miracle. Another small one. Not of *The Magic Flute* or London Philharmonic variety.

Just another note, any note, besides "*pffjl-luuugghhh.*"

WHY
CATALOGUES
WERE INVENTED

—೨

Want to get rich fast?

You could, you know. Just come up with a way to take the pain and frustration out of spring shopping with children.

Think about it.

Have you watched a mother with a teenage daughter hunting for her first prom dress? Or a second-grade son buying a scout uniform? Or a three-year-old in the shoe department?

The first is a battle of bulges; the second of wits; and the third is the stuff of which Purple Hearts are made.

It sounds so simple: mother and child off on a fun

shopping afternoon. Maybe stop for a Coke somewhere. Have a nice talk.

Ha.

There may be a blue-sky beginning, but thunder clouds lurk behind every coatrack and sock bin. The only hint of a rainbow comes as faces turn from pink to red and—when Mom reads the price tag—a budget-busted white.

Part of the problem, of course, is not the designer of clothes, but the designer of children, for, like the clothes they wear (or don't wear), children come in many different styles.

Mercurial Muriel   This kind of kid either loves or hates things on sight. Trouble is, she never runs 100 percent on any one thing. She loves the jacket, but hates the hood. In a package of four somethings, she likes one. Can't live without it. When the clothes have finally been selected, tax figured, check written, shopping bag stuffed—she pulls on Mom's arm and says, "I've changed my mind."

No-Rear Roy   No matter what brand of jeans his mother buys, it's the Fruit of the Loom label that shows. He refuses to wear a belt, but his problem might be solved if little boy's pants came in husky, regular, slim, and concave.

Bashful Belinda   She always locks the dressing-room door and insists that everyone stand outside.

When she's ready, Mom can come to the door and peek. Only Mom. She never speaks above a whisper, but does a lot of tugging at the coattails and rolling her eyes. She treats all salespersons like lepers, and would absolutely have an aneurysm if anyone in the store knew she had just bought a you-know-what.

Toreador Tom Dive-bombing through the shirt racks, shinnying up the display shelves, whooping up the down escalator, he judges clothes by the kind of thing Batman or Muscle Man would wear. His mom's face twitches as she mumbles quiet obscenities, and store clerks have been known to turn in their resignation after he leaves.

Clotheshorse Carol This teenager never puts off 'til tomorrow anything she can put on today. She wears clothes out, but never more than once, and finding needles in haystacks is a piece of cake compared to finding the Perfect Jeans or the Right Shoes. She has closets crammed with clothes, but nothing to wear. Take socks, for example. She wants a complete collection: tennis socks, Sunday socks, tube socks, knee socks, running socks, plain socks, textured socks, sheer socks, opaque socks, short socks, long socks, plaid socks, appliquéd socks, tasseled socks, thin socks, thick socks, cotton socks, woolen socks, colored socks, white socks, double-thick socks, extra-sheer socks. And then?

Then she wears sneakers with no socks.

Mud Pie Mac A real challenge, this guy always manages to get clothes dirty, even when he's just trying them on. His scabby knees shine through the tough-skin, guaranteed, reinforced, childproof, double-thick pants. He has holy-moly runs in all his knit shirts. He eats collars, picks threads, bites off buttons. He tortures pockets to death, stuffing them with rocks, Matchbox cars, Magic Markers, Jell-O mix, dead flowers until they, poor things, just come apart at the seams. It's important to select clothes for him that look good inside out and backward.

Tacky Tish Her clothes represent more dollars than sense. She's into platform shoes, six-inch heels, and all other fashions that leave Mom biting her tongue until it bleeds. Flipping through a rack of dresses, she and Mom never slow down at the same place. Dress-up means clean jeans and a Jefferson Starship T-shirt. At three, she likes wrap skirts that won't stay wrapped and at thirteen, she likes miniskirts and glow-in-the-dark mascara. There's no use arguing with her and telling her she looks silly. She'll just go hunt up Mom's high school annual as Exhibit A to show that what some people call silly, other people call style.

Grover Grouch This one never can be found when it's time to go shopping. He hates trying on clothes. He hates holding hands through the parking lot. He hates trailing behind Mom through the mall. He hates being told not to pick leaves off the philodendron in the furniture department. He sputters, breathes heavy, and crosses his eyes in protest if Mom even slows down, much less stops to browse, in the ladies department. His answer to everything from "Do you like it?" to "Does it fit?" is, "Yeah. Can I take it off now?"

He especially hates having pants fitted. Not standing on one foot, not stepping on the alteration-lady's fingers, not having to go to the bathroom in the middle of the whole ordeal is just not his style.

Everything he tries on seems either to scratch, feel slippery, choke, bulge, or is, in his words, just stupid looking. In shoe stores, he waits until the clerk has blown up, tied, and handed him his free balloon. Then he says, "I want a blue one."

Once, coming home bankrupt and berserk from a shopping trip during which our children could have been easily mistaken for the Goodall chimps, I asked them to go to their room and lay out their very favorite outfit.

Four-year-old Claire selected her swim team sweatshirt and a pair of my high heels. McNair, then eight, chose the mop-head-and-kitchen-apron outfit left over from her Raggedy Ann Halloween, and George, nine, sat empty-handed, saying he couldn't find anything he really liked.

I rest my case.

TALKING
MACHINES

‑‑‑ා

*H*ello. *You have reached the Hughs residence. We can't
come to the phone right now, but if you leave your name
and number at the sound of the tone, we'll get back with
you as soon as we can.*

"Mom, this is Claire. I have these awful pains in
my stomach, and I almost fainted in chemistry class.
Call me when you come in. 'Bye."

*Hi there! Boy, do you have the right number! This is
Claire and Meredith's room. We're out having a wild and
crazy time with rich fraternity guys. Unless you are our
parents. If you are our parents, we are both in the library
working on our Phi Beta Kappa research project. But, whoever you are, near or far . . . oooh wee ohhh wah*

*wah . . . when you hear the tone, rap in the phone . . .
doo dee dah dah doo dee dah.*

"Claire, this is Mom. I thought you were sick! I
don't like that phone message. It's . . . well . . .
besides, it's too long. I'm glad you are well enough
to go out. If you feel bad tomorrow, go to the
infirmary."

*Hello. You have reached the Hughs residence. We can't
come to the phone right now, but if you leave your name
and number at the sound of the tone, we'll get back with
you as soon as we can.*

"Hey, Mom. This is George. Guess what? Friday
classes were canceled, and I got someone to work
for me this weekend, so I'm coming home. See you
in a couple of hours. I'm bringing four friends. Wait!
I forgot. There'll be five. Six, counting me. Don't
go to any trouble."

*Hello. You have reached the Hughs residence. We can't
come to the phone right now, but if you leave your name
and number at the sound of the tone, we'll get back with
you as soon as we can.*

"Mom, it's me again. I feel awful, but I can't go
to the infirmary. They don't know anything. I got
these green-looking pills from a girl down the hall
whose uncle is a doctor and gave them to her when
she had mono, but we're not sure how many to take.
Everybody says they're positive it's mono. I definitely have fever. Meredith said she'd never felt such

a hot forehead, and I'm *sooooooo* tired. Call as soon as you come in. I'm going to bed. Oh, we changed the message. 'Bye."

Hello. If you have a message for Claire or Meredith, leave it at the sound of the tone.

"Claire? *Claire!* Claire, wake up! Hello? *Hello!* Is anybody there? There may be a sick sleeping child with advanced mono who is in a coma and needs her mother!!!"

Hello. You have reached the Hughs residence. We can't come to the phone right now, but if you leave your name and number at the sound of the tone, we'll get back with you as soon as we can.

"Mom, this is McNair. Uh. Hmmmm. Does the car insurance cover cracks in the windshield? . . . Like from pebbles that get thrown up and hit the window? It's kind of a big crack. Maybe it was more like a rock. I mean, it's not that big. I've got a piece of cardboard over it, but it's raining. Um. Well, never mind. Don't worry. 'Bye."

Hello. You have reached the Hughs residence. We can't come to the phone right now, but if you leave your name and number at the sound of the tone, we'll get back with you as soon as we can.

"Mom? I got your message. It was embarrassing. Don't scream in the phone like that. I think I was just tired. I feel better now. Don't bother calling back. This is beach weekend. Oh, could you send me McNair's black short strapless for the prom? I need it tomorrow night. Thanks. 'Bye."

Hello. You have reached the Hughs residence. We can't come to the phone right now, but if you leave your name and number at the sound of the tone, we'll get back with you as soon as we can.

"Mom. This is George. I forgot my house key. We're at . . . Hey, what's the name of this place? . . . Exit 360 Quick 'n Go . . . something like that. Call us . . . well no. We'll just call back. 'Bye. Wait! I almost forgot. There are eight of us. 'Bye."

Hello. You have reached the Hughs residence. We have bashed our answering machine with an ax. We don't want anymore messages. So, when you hear the sound of the tone, hang up, and call someone else. 'Bye.

DAUGHTERS
WHO CARE
TOO MUCH

—໑

Sometimes you wonder where talk-show hosts dig up such weird guests. I've not led a completely sheltered life, but I've never met anyone who thinks she is Cleopatra, and I never realized there were such things as men who used to be women married to women who used to be men.

Last week, I read where Sally Jessy Raphael was featuring "daughters embarrassed by their mothers' appearance or behavior."

Now that I can relate to.

I didn't catch the show, but Raphael probably had a run on eligible mother-daughter pairs. In fact, I don't know a mother worth the title who hasn't made her daughter's eyes roll heavenward at some point. Probably lots of points.

My own daughters stayed mortified for years at a time. How did I embarrass them? Let me count the ways:

They lived in dread that I would actually open my mouth and say something when driving car pool. Mothers were to be seen and not heard.

"Just hush up and drive, Mom," their squinty eyes screamed whenever I cleared my throat to speak.

When I refused to start the engine until everyone was buckled in, they died of embarrassment. When I was late, they died of embarrassment. When I was early, they died of embarrassment. Even when I was on time, just the fact that I was there was embarrassing.

They sought sympathy from their friends when I refused to let them wear boxer shorts to the church picnic. When I said no to getting their ears pierced, they would have put themselves up for adoption if given half a chance.

"You cannot pierce your ears until you are twelve," I said.

According to them, I was the only mother in captivity who hadn't taken her daughter down to the jewelry store when they were still in Pampers.

But all these were mere skirmishes compared with the embarrassment over getting their driver's licenses.

Or, I should say, not getting them until they actually learned to drive.

The rule in our house was that you had to learn to drive a gearshift car well enough to take the test in it. None of this jumping out of bed on their six-teenth birthdays and, after a lucky turn around the block with some sleepy policeman, being let loose on the highway.

Getting an old, asthmatic Volkswagen stick shift to behave tends to make one a more careful driver. It's hard to scratch off on a hill, and you have to slow down around curves if you want to keep from stalling. Poor babies. While all their friends (to hear them talk) had brand-new, fire-engine-red cars of their very own, they had to stay in my good graces so they could borrow a dirty gray Dasher that smelled like dog breath and didn't even have power steering.

It wasn't just my behavior that embarrassed them. My appearance brought them gobs of shame. All I had to do was appear.

My notes on the backs of their report cards were embarrassing. Trimming the crust off their sand-wiches, practicing with them on how to shake hands and look people in the eye—everything was embar-rassing.

Showing up for Mother's Day at school was em-barrassing. Not showing up was embarrassing.

For years, I made their lives miserable no matter what I wore. In my fake-leopard-fur-coat stage, they said I looked like Tammy Bakker. In my black boots, they said I looked like an aging, overweight Barbie.

It's a wonder they survived me.

Just the other day, our youngest, home from college for the weekend, was leaving to drive back when I saw that old familiar look again: eyeballs rolled back, hands on hips, a long "Oh, Mom . . ." leaving her limp, and tapping her foot.

All I said was, "Don't you think you need a coat? Promise you'll not go over sixty. I cut you some oranges to snack on in the car. When was the last time you changed your oil? Are you sure you aren't catching a cold? How much sleep are you getting? Did you balance your checkbook? Have you written your thank-you notes? All that loud music will ruin your ears, and call us when you get there."

RESOLVING (AGAIN)

‿つ

Wh" hat will we see, and who will we be in the New Year?

No one really knows, of course. Tea leaves, statistics, trends—it's all a guessing game. As we tack the new calendar on the wall, with its 365 blank squares, the best we can do is to recheck our resolutions and wishes for the days ahead. Here are some of mine:

I resolve (again) to exercise more, eat less, and control my temper.

To pay cash.

To look people in the face when I talk.

To laugh at myself, think things through.

To live my intentions, speak my convictions.
To pick my fights carefully.

To write letters like in the olden days, so someday, my childen's children's children can analyze my
handwriting and hear a voice they never heard ear-
to-ear.

Not only to smell more roses, but to help plant
them. Also yellow tulips. Maybe even occasionally
to rake leaves.

Not to let a single houseplant die of thirst.

I promise to bug out of my grown children's lives
even though I am full of wise, wonderful, expert,
free, ever-ready advice that could make them perfect
and happy forever and ever.

I will listen more than I talk.

Control my greed in bookstores and record shops.

Not covet my neighbor's hair.

Not give almond croissants, yeast rolls, and anything coconut more power than they deserve.

I promise to speak up when I hear jokes that aren't
really funny.

I will be more interested in truth than in facts.

What do I wish for in the New Year?

I wish places like Somalia and Bosnia needed
Weight Watchers and freezer bags for leftovers.

That Madonna's book and Rush Limbaugh's program couldn't draw a crowd.

That people would stop ridiculing and terrorizing

people because of whom they love in the privacy of their own lives.

That we would all listen to the words we say in church and try harder to live what they mean. And let God be the judge of who is doing it better.

I wish little children already born into this world had advocates as energetic and resourceful as those who might be born.

For all of us to remember that people on the outside of our circles, those who are the targets of our insults and our prejudices, all have names, a right to be different, and the image of the same God on their DNA.

That nobody can think of a single good reason to kill a whale, buy an assault weapon, have a baby unless they can love and take care of it, start smoking, throw trash on the highway, or take more than their share of anything.

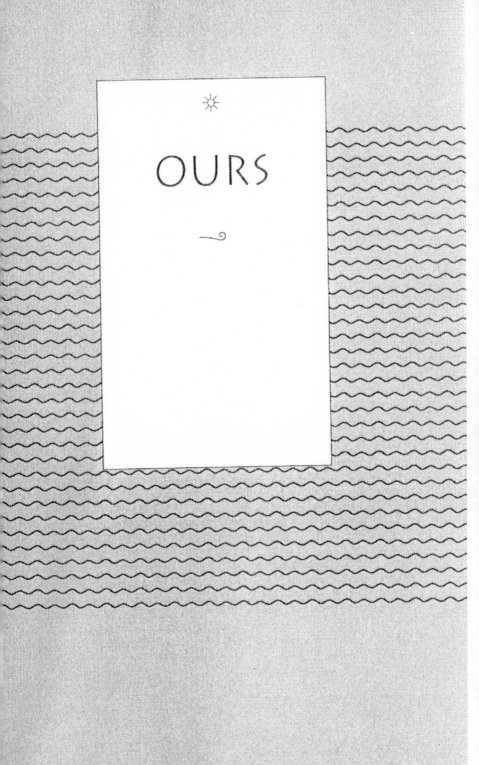

OURS

*S*ome people say children should be seen and not heard. Some people don't give them enough credit for what they can teach us.

A kid once asked her Sunday-school teacher how come the children of Israel had to do all the work: It was the children of Israel who built the ark, crossed the Red Sea, found their way to the Promised Land.

"Didn't the grown-ups do anything?"

One thing we grown-ups need to do more of is to listen to our children, to learn through them, and with them.

Way back when—a phrase we like to use when time has played tricks and we wonder where it all went—my son was giving his little sister a hard time. We were sitting at the dinner table and she had a surprise to announce to the family.

"Guess what," she said. "I learned something really hard today. Something important."

Her dad and I waited anxiously for the big news, but her brother wasn't impressed. He just rolled his eyes.

"My ABC's. I learned my ABC's. I can say them all."

Before she could get going on them, her brother zipped from A to Z fast as he could. Her face fell, but she was not to be overdone. She stuck her chin up in the air, looked him straight in the eyes and said, "Well, you may know yours, but you don't know mine."

Yours. Mine. We're all in this together, you know.

It's the only way we'll make it to the Promised Land.

MCDARN-ITS

⎯Ↄ

"WELCOME TO MCDONALD'S DRIVE-
THROUGH WINDOW. MAY I TAKE YOUR
ORDER, PLEASE?"

"We'd like one hamburger, plain, one with mustard and ketchup, a double with cheese—"

"No, Dad, I don't want any mustard, I hate mustard."

"Make that one with just ketchup, three fries."

"SMALL OR LARGE?"

"Medium."

"I'M SORRY. WE HAVE ONLY SMALL OR
LARGE."

"Small."

"Large. Please, Dad, pleeeeez."

"OK. Three large fries."

"Mom says she wants just a small."

"Uh, make that one small and one large. And one chicken nuggets."

"SIX, NINE, TWELVE, OR TWENTY-FOUR?"

"Just one."

"I'M SORRY, SIR. WE CAN'T SELL JUST ONE CHICKEN NUGGET. THEY COME IN BOXES OF SIX, NINE, TWELVE—"

"One order. One order of nuggets."

"WHAT SIZE, SIR?"

"I'm sorry. I can't hear you."

"WHAT SIZE CHICKEN NUGGETS DO YOU WANT?"

"Large, I guess."

"THAT'S ONE HAMBURGER, PLAIN, ONE WITH JUST KETCHUP, ONE DOUBLE CHEESE, A TWENTY-FOUR CHICKEN NUGGETS—"

"Twenty-four? I can't eat twenty-four pieces of chicken!"

Honk-honk . . .

"WOULD YOU LIKE TO TRY THE MEDIUM NUGGETS, NINE PIECES?"

"Yeah, gimme that."

"THAT'S ONE HAMBURGER, PLAIN,

ONE WITH JUST KETCHUP, ONE DOUBLE CHEESE, ONE MEDIUM NUGGETS, THREE LARGE, TWO SMALL FRIES."

"No, *two* large and *one* small fry. Er, fries."

"THAT'S ONE HAMBURGER, PLAIN, ONE WITH JUST KETCHUP, ONE DOUBLE CHEESE, ONE MEDIUM NUGGETS, THREE LARGE, TWO SMALL—NO, WAIT, I'M SORRY, THAT'S TWO LARGE, ONE SMALL FRIES. WILL THAT BE ALL, SIR?"

"Yes, thank God."

"Dad! What about drinks?"

"Miss?? Hello!! Hey Miss, don't go yet, please."

Honk-honk. "Hey, Buddy, what's going on up there? If you want Thanskgiving dinner, you gotta go inside."

"May we add something to drink? Uh, we'll take two small Pepsis—"

"I'M SORRY, WE ONLY HAVE COKE."

"I want a Sprite, Dad."

"SIR, WE HAVE ORANGE, DIET COKE, COKE, COFFEE, TEA, WATER, SPRITE, AND DR PEPPER."

"OK. We'll take a medium orange, a small coffee, a Diet Coke, and a Sprite."

"Awww. Did she say they had Dr Pepper, Dad?"

"Can we get a sundae, Dad? You promised on the way over here."

"Miss . . . uh . . . heh, heh . . . could you just change the Sprite to a Dr Pepper and add three more chocolate sundaes, please?"

"WITH OR WITHOUT NUTS?"

"With."

"Without. I don't like nuts."

"Scrape them off."

"BEG YOUR PARDON?"

"Nothing. Never mind."

"SIR, ARE YOU SAYING YOU WOULD LIKE TO CANCEL YOUR ORDER?"

Honk-honk . . .

"No. Please don't go away. We've got it now. That's all. We're all fixed up."

"I want a cherry pie instead of a sundae. How come they get a sundae and I don't get a pie and I don't even want a sundae?"

"THAT'S ONE HAMBURGER, PLAIN, ONE WITH KETCHUP, ONE DOUBLE CHEESE, ONE MEDIUM NUGGETS, TWO LARGE, ONE SMALL FRIES, A MEDIUM ORANGE, A SMALL COFFEE, A DIET COKE, A DR PEPPER AND THREE CHOCOLATE SUNDAES. YOUR ORDER COMES TO TEN DOLLARS AND FORTY-SEVEN CENTS. PLEASE PAY AT THE WINDOW."

"Dad? Dad! What's the matter?"

"I forgot my wallet."

SCENT-AMENTAL
JOURNEYS

—ᴐ

Even in Birkenstocks, an old rag sweater, and hiker's hair—a mother is a mother is a mother. Despite my disguise, the seat-assigners at USAir knew a veteran of the trenches when they saw one, and I'm convinced that's why they put me, traveling alone on the long flight home from a rafting vacation on the Colorado River, between a sixteen-month-old and a four-year-old, behind a two-year-old, and across the aisle from an airsick father with a pale green toddler.

By the time I got home, I'd relived those nightmare trips in the car back when our kids were little. Taking them anywhere took courage, a sense of humor, a bag of bribes, and a mental replay of our marriage vows.

"When are we gonna get there?"

"Make him stop picking on me."

"I'm hot."

"I'm cold."

"Mama, my mouth is watering. I feel sick."

And we wouldn't even be out of the driveway.

Like I said, motherly types seem to send off some kind of bleep. The kid in front knew I'd be a good sport when he reached over the seat, took a swat at my coffee cup, and dumped it into my backpack.

The man across the aisle knew, somehow, that, yes, I would be glad to hold his child while he went to the bathroom and that, no, it wouldn't hurt my feelings when the kid looked at me like I was Jack the Ripper, screamed for me to let him loose, told the whole planeload of people that he did not like me, and then threw up. On me.

The sixteen-month-old next to me knew that when she got tired of her grape juice and applesauce, she could just spit them in my lap. She even decided to put her chewing gum on my nose when it lost its flavor.

And when she lost her cookies, so to speak, she naturally looked my way.

It was a very rough flight.

But, then, traveling with kids is always rough. How many times can you sing "Little Bunny Foo Foo" without going nuts? I remember well those endless drives to Georgia to spend Thanksgiving with my husband's family, way back when.

I'd beg him to let me drive. But, no.

"I don't mind," he'd say bravely.

When we finally drove in the driveway, my hair was pulled out by the roots, my lap sore from being jumped on, arms paralyzed from holding sleeping heads. Lollipops stuck to my shoes, game pieces and crumbs itched all down the front of my blouse, and nobody wanted to even touch the wet washrag we always traveled with.

Usually, whoever needed it had been sitting in my lap when they needed it.

My mother-in-law would take one look at us getting out of the car and get that poor-baby look on her face as she helped my husband to the door.

"Ohhhhhh. You look so tired, son. Come in and rest here on the sofa while Ina puts the children down, brings you some iced tea, fans your face, wipes your feet, pats your hand . . . you mean you drove all the way? I bet you are exhausted!"

I'm kidding, of course. It wasn't that bad. I really didn't have to fix the iced tea. Just bring it to him.

Once, when the children were something like

three, five, and six, even *he* lost it. They kept asking and kept asking, "How much longer?" and "Are we almost there?"

After the eleven-hundredth time, he turned around and pointed his finger while I grabbed the wheel. "DON'T ASK ME ONE MORE TIME HOW MANY MORE MILES OR IF WE ARE ALMOST THERE. JUST DON'T ASK."

Silence in the backseat. Absolute silence.

Then, a little voice:

"Dad? Just tell me this. How old will I be when we get there?"

I didn't actually grow old on my plane trip home from Arizona, but as I got my welcome-back hug, my husband wanted to know, "What's that smell?"

Why should he recognize it?

A
MOTHER'S-DAY
SHOOTOUT

—❧

Motherhood and guns don't seem to go together, unless maybe it's for a *Saturday Night Live* skit or a Stephen King movie. But considering the stories we read, the shootings we watch, and the fact that other countries are handing out survival kits to warn our visitors—getting reasonably serious and seriously reasonable about violence American style may be the best gift we mothers can give ourselves.

One of the books tucked in my backpack on vacation last summer was a colletion of short stories called *Flash Fiction*. Among the stories, one titled "Jane" is about a young woman trying to deal with her sister's abortion. The dynamics of this decision

≈

and its impact on the family are told in sharp, probing prose. The name of its author stuck in my mind: Steven Molen. Partly, I guess, because I was interested that it was written by a man through the eyes of a woman.

So when I came across the name Steven Molen in an article in *Utne Reader,* it got my attention. So did the title of the article: "Another Mother's Child."

It was a reprint of a letter Norma Molen wrote to her son Steven after he had been killed by a handgun. By the time I read his story, Steven had been dead about two months.

Steven was in graduate school pursuing a promising career after having been picked up by a major publisher while still in college. On April 23, 1993, Steven went to meet his girlfriend, Susan Clements, who lived in the women's wing of the dormitory they both shared. As the two of them left, Andreas Drexler, an ex-boyfriend of Susan's, came out of nowhere, shot Susan three times in the face, and Steven once in the stomach. Later that night, grieving over what sudden anger had made him do, Drexler killed himself. Susan died instantly. Machines kept Steven alive for five days.

That Mother's Day, only days after burying her son, Norma Molen stood on the steps of the Lincoln Memorial as part of a grass-roots rally against gun violence. I had read Steven's story, not knowing any of this. Steven's story ends with Jane being frightened by noises she hears in the empty house after her parents have left to take her sister to the hospital. She hears a door open somewhere in the emptiness, then, "soft like the branches on my window before a storm," come footsteps on the stairs. Who was it? Was it a ghost baby? Jane wonders.

No. It is Jane's parents, coming to her rescue.

Which is exactly what Norma Molen was doing when she went to Washington on Mother's Day to read her letter aloud, the letter she wrote to Steven after he died. She was coming, if not to his rescue, then to the rescue of other sons and daughters who die useless deaths, every day, in cities all across the country. She was trying to shake other mothers out of our dangerous sleep and our idiotic mind games about what gun violence is doing to our children.

She had come to rescue children from the noises on the steps.

Here is part of that letter:

> There is no legitimate need for a handgun in a civilized society, a technology designed specifically for killing, a weapon for a coward. And we, like most Americans, were lethargic about this grotesque carnage until you became a victim, not in a drug war, but on the fourteenth floor of the graduate dormitory at Indiana University. The killing is everywhere—twenty-

five thousand last year. And more people arm themselves each day because we have allowed the gun industry to promote a solution of complete madness. In civilized countries, people don't buy handguns. The only exception in European countries is for members of target-shooting societies, but the gun is never taken from the range.

Norma Molen ends her letter with the suggestion that a wall like the Vietnam Memorial be built in front of the Capitol. On it would be recorded the names of victims killed in their own land because their senators and representatives did not have the integrity and common sense to establish laws that would protect the public.

If lawmakers continue to pay more allegiance to powerful lobbies than to our young people in suburbs and ghettos, then maybe it's time mothers come to the rescue.

After all, that's our job.

SUMMER FUN

—ᴐ

Summertime is when the living gets easy. Or so the song says. Certainly, things at work tend to slow down during July and August, but summertime is a busy time for play.

Especially for kids.

The most memorable projects of my childhood were almost all done during the summer months, when getting up early was a lot easier, because it was off to play instead of off to school. After supper, the sun stayed out late enough to get in a couple more hours of hard fun, and even in the hot noonday sun, when the rule was to come in and rest awhile, there were a host of no-homework kinds of things to do:

Blanket and card-table forts. Listening in on the phone when your older sister called her friends. Eating butter straight out of the ice box. Dressing up the dog. Playing rock-paper-scissors and slapjack.

But the real fun was outside.

Like the summer you and your best friend Sally built the raft. It took a whole month to find enough scraps of wood, to argue over what went where, and how you could convince your parents to let you pack a lunch and float down the inland waterway for a couple of days.

Actually, that turned out to be a moot point, because it took about three seconds for the thing to sink to the bottom the first time you put in. Somehow it didn't matter, though. You dragged it out and turned it into a raceway for the fiddler crabs you caught and lined up, giving them each a name. You even dabbled in the gambling business that summer. Bunches of other kids of various ages would gather around the dead boat and, using buttons from your mother's. sewing box, place bets on which crabs would cross the finish line (formerly the rudder) before the others.

Then there were the drama productions.

Not until your own children sold make-believe tickets to their backyard driveway musicals and magic shows did you realize how truly wonderful those productions were.

Or how much mess they made.

A few years ago, when lip-syncing became so popular with the MTV crowd, little did they know that you and Sally invented it years ago in the basement of her house, behind locked doors and pulled curtains so no boys could spy. You'd put on a Joni James or Johnny Ray record and sync your hearts out into the juice-can microphone.

The other night, your two grown daughters went through their repertoire of cheerleading cheers they spent one whole summer learning with their cousins on rainy afternoons under the beach-house porch. That was, one confessed, the summer she'd narrowed it down to being either a missionary or a cheerleader for the Dallas Cowboys when she grew up.

In hearing about all the good mischief your children got themselves into filling up those delicious summer days of childhood, you wondered where you were while they were doing it. Like the time they took turns shutting each other up in suitcases and being pushed down the steps.

It was their rendition of Niagara Falls in a barrel.

Anybody who has trouble with evolution need only take a stroll down memory lane and then through the modern-day toy store. Water toys alone take up several aisles. You and Sally used to squirt under the hose—a plain and simple garden hose. You'd use it for a jump rope, or stick it down the front of your bathing suits and make water-balloon bosoms.

Kids don't have to imagine anything anymore.

They don't have to build rafts or rob their mother's button box or go over the "rapids" in a suitcase. They have things like Shout and Shoot voice-activated water guns; Nerf Liquidator Bats; Sonic Splash Zoom balls; Mighty Morphin Power Rangers.

Reckon they're as much fun as a stable of crabs and a button bookie?

HOMESICK
REVISITED

—☺

It started with a lump in your throat and then moved down in your rib cage.

Like your heart had gained weight. Like you'd suddenly been tossed overboard into a sea of strange faces, bugles blowing at all hours, and no television.

The catalogue was wrong. The brochures were wrong. You thought summer camp would be the land of milk and honey, giggles and sunshine, new best friends and so much to do, you would forget to write home.

But as you stood there, watching the taillights of the family car get smaller and smaller down the dusty road, you knew you were a condemned person.

A lost soul.

The place smelled like mildew and fresh-cut grass. There were charts that told you when to eat and where to put your laundry on what day. You couldn't figure out where the mail room was or how ten people could use the same bathroom. What if everybody had to go at the same time? All at once? What then?

While you were trying to figure that one out, a bell rang, and you didn't know what that meant, so you decided to go back to your cabin. But you couldn't remember exactly which one it was.

Things only got worse at supper, in a dining hall full of people who knew the words to songs you had never heard and wore T-shirts from places you'd never been.

They gulped down glasses of "bug juice" and lumps of spaghetti. What *is* bug juice? Does it come from bugs? Is there some way to ask and make it sound like a joke? Like you really knew the answer?

You poked at your food and your eyes watered. What were those little brown slimy things? They looked like mushrooms. The spillover came when you thought about Mom. *Her* spaghetti never has mushrooms. *She* knows you don't like them.

You wonder if it is possible for a person to blow her nose and wipe her eyes at a table with eight weird people staring at her and not be seen.

You went to your cabin and your unmade bed and its mountain of neatly folded clothes with your name tagged on every collar and waistband. How could people learn your name if it was written in the inside of your clothes? You had a whole duffel bag full of towels but had no idea where the showers were.

The evening program was a skit on all the different activities to choose from tomorrow. Waking up in your own room at home was not among them.

You tried to act like you were having fun because if you didn't, some counselor would come and take you aside, asking questions like, "Is something bothering you?" and "Don't you want to talk about it?"

Yes, there was something bothering you, but the only people who could have helped just hauled your trunk up the hill, told you to remember to brush your teeth, kissed you with a tight little smile, and drove off into the sunset.

Before bedtime that first night, you only thought you were going to die. After Taps, you knew you were.

Tomorrow, there were Red Cross swimming tests to pass, and you had never swum in a dark, creepy lake.

The blanket on the top bunk hung down like the giant wings on a bat, and pine trees wheezed outside like they were alive and plotting.

How could you stand it until Closing Day?

Granddaddy longlegs in the rafters. Mushrooms in the spaghetti. What next?

And suppose your mother died while you were away, and nobody told you. Suppose your mail is censored. Suppose some night you got sick and threw up on the cabin floor?

˙Suppose you wet the bed?

You wonder what Mom and Dad are doing at home.

Someday, after you have ironed on a wad of name tags, squeezed a dozen towels into a duffel, gagged down a sob with a quick kiss, and blown your nose all the way down a dusty road, you'll know.

There's only one thing worse than being homesick for your mother, and that's *being* your mother.

PARANOID
PICASSOS

—૭

Ever wondered what those blobs of wet, dripping paint the kids bring home from Sunday school or first grade mean? Is there some hidden message stuck in there somewhere under the gummy glitter and paste-on stars?

Parents today have been warned by a chorus of child-raising experts that you never come right out and ask, "What in the heck is that supposed to be?" It may be a perfectly logical, innocent question, one we are *supposed* to ask in museums and art galleries —but woe to the mama who is so unthinking she ruins her children with such a brutal question. It might hurt their feelings. Just hang it on the refrig-

erator and wait until the mood strikes the artist to
elaborate.

Back in the olden days, before *parent* became a
verb and there weren't so many experts telling us
what to do, mamas and daddies didn't beat around
the bush. When kids came home with their con-
struction paper love offerings, they asked what it was.
When neighbors came over and saw something black
and purple with six eyes and half a box of macaroni
pasted around it hanging on the refrigerator, Mother
knew what to say.

"What is that?"

"Oh, that's one of the plagues of Egypt."

How do you know these things unless you ask? It
might just as well be a self-portrait, and then look
what you've done.

It's sad that mamas today can't come right out and
ask. I have found Jesus in a number of disguises, but
I would never have seen him in the painted clothespin our son brought home one Sunday if I hadn't
forgotten myself for a moment and just come right
out and asked.

"Why on earth are you kissing that clothespin?"

"It's the Baby Jesus," he said proudly.

If I had asked, as I later learned you were supposed
to, "Son, would you like to tell me about this?" he
would have shrugged and said, "No. I'd rather have
a Popsicle."

There's even a book written about how to look at your child's art, what question to ask, and what it all means. The title is downright intimidating: *Mommy, Daddy, Look What I'm Saying: What Your Children Are Telling You Through Their Art.* It is a scary book for parents like me who didn't take abnormal psychology and might be missing some clues.

Frankly, I think folks are getting a little paranoid.

The chapter on "Common Warning Signs" is the stuff of nightmares. It says shaky lines, inconsistencies, unrecognizable objects are just a few of the "danger signs" children give in their artwork. The case-history pictures drawn by kids who have gone zonkers or grow up to become ax murderers look no different from the ones that used to hang on our refrigerator and are now stuck in scrapbooks up in the attic.

"Slanted images at any age need to be investigated," the book warns.

Uh-oh. One Christmas, our three children collaborated on a drawing of the whole family which I framed and gave to their grandparents. We all slant in that picture. The house slants. The dog slants. Some of the trees grow right off the side of the page, where our three-year-old planted them with her slanted green crayon.

"Slant" is good in art. Picasso slants like crazy. Who are these people telling me that my children's picture should be hanging in some shrink's office instead of on their grandparents' bedroom wall?

I like the story of the little girl who said she was drawing a picture of God.

"You can't draw a picture of God," the teacher told her. "Nobody knows what God looks like."

"Well," said the child, "they will when I get through."

DRIVEN
TO
DISTRACTION

—☽

Ever played "Twenty Questions" with a four-year-old?

Pick one. It can be your own, a niece or nephew, a grandchild, a neighbor. Four-year-olds are not shy if you give them half a chance. Put him or her next to you in the front seat of the car, turn off the radio, and start driving.

First one question, then another. And another. And another. And another. And another. It goes something like this:

"How much does a tree weigh?"

"I don't know."

"What does it feel like to be a worm?"

"I don't know."

"Did you ask a lot of questions when you were little?"

"Yes."

"Then how come you don't know anything?"

"I'll try harder. Ask me something else."

"Are all skies blue?"

"Yes."

"How do you know? Have you seen them all? Maybe way over yonder the sky is green and the grass is blue. Maybe, huh?"

"It's all one sky. It's all hooked together. God probably thought about other colors, but I think he ended up with the right choice, don't you?"

"Nope. I would have colored the sky GREEN and the grass PURPLE. Do you think God might ever change his mind? Huh? Are you listening?"

"I'm thinking, I'm thinking. Sometimes God does change the colors of the sky. Have you ever seen him do that?"

"You mean like sunsets? Once, when we left the tent up in the backyard, the grass under it turned brown."

"It's nice of God to make colors change, don't you think?"

"Yeah, but it sure made my daddy mad about the grass."

"Do you like to ride in the car?"

"Yeah. What makes the car drive?"

"Well—"

"Is it fun to drive?"

"Well—"

"What is the hardest thing about driving?"

"Well—"

"Do you get tired of driving?"

"Well—"

"Can I drive?"

"No."

"Riding in the car for a long time makes my weer hurt."

"Your what?"

"Weer. You know. The back part of your lap."

"Driving makes my *rrr*-ear hurt."

"Mine too."

"No, I mean it's *rrr* instead of *www*. Want some gum? Here's a big piece. Chew that for a while."

"Wham ard reersh madove?"

"Don't try to talk and chew at the same time."

"What are rears made of?"

"Same thing as shoulders and arms."

"What are shoulders and arms made of?"

"Calcium and marrow."

"What is calcium and marrow made of?"

"Uh, metallic components and blood, I think."

"What's blood ma—"

"Hey! I got an idea. Why don't you tell me some answers and I will try to come up with the right question. Ever played that before?"

"You mean like Jeopardy?"

"Sure. Like *Jeopardy*."

"OK. The . . . answer . . . is . . . ummmmm . . .
A HUNDRED TWO ZILLION KABILLION."

"Is that how tall the sky is?"

"Nope."

"How many stars there are?"

"Nope."

"I give up."

"It's how old you are. Ha ha ha ha ha Ha ha ha Ha
ha ha ha ha ha Ha ha ha Ha ha ha ha ha ha . . ."

WORKING
MOTHERS AND
DAUGHTERS

—♋

Every afternoon at about three-thirty, phones in offices all over America ring. Women pick them up and hear something like this:

"Hey, Mom. It's me.

"Yeah, I got home all right. I'm hungry, but there's nothing here.

"Lunch? I threw it away. The sandwich was green. But I don't like cucumber sandwiches. Can I have some brownies?

"Well, then, I'll just eat the mix out of the box. Yes, I can. With a spoon.

"Oh, I almost forget. The sink is bubbling and gross. It has junk floating all in it.

"The English test? I forget exactly what I made.

Besides, Mom, I have to have some poster paper right now. It's for a big grade tomorrow. I have to have it now. This minute. Oh, by the way, the gerbil is loose. Can we have tacos for supper? And guess who's watching *General Hospital*, even though you told him he couldn't? Want me to beat on him for you, huh? Just kidding.

"Mom, can't I please take my peanut butter and apple to the attic and play—just this once? I'll be careful. No roaches will come.

"Why? Wait! Don't hang up. Can you ask around to see if anyone there wants Girl Scout cookies? I'll hold. Why can't you?

"Well, can I invite a friend over?

"Why?

"Can I build a fire?

"Why?

"Can we buy an Atari?

"Why?

"Mom, somebody called and said to call back. We owed them money or something like that. I don't know. There wasn't a pencil.

"Can I borrow your nail polish?

"Why?

"The sink is making noises, Mom. It's fuller than it was when I came in. It looks like someone got sick in it. I'm not putting my hands in that junk, Mom!

"Mom, tell him to stop hitting me. He's hitting me. You are, too, you creep. . . .

"Mom, when are you coming home?

"What do you mean, *never* . . . *MOM!*

"*MOM!?*"

GIFTS
WORTH
CLAIMING

─૭

There's a new term in education that gives me the willies every time I hear it: gifted.

Sometimes it's got a double whammy: gifted and talented.

Books I read on the subject, written by so-called experts in education, make me even more depressed. They try to convince us that the future of our society depends on singling out these little cultural messiahs from the unblessed.

The term has certainly caught on. There's the National Foundation for Gifted and Creative Children; World Council for the Gifted; and a Gifted and Talented division within the U.S. Office of Education. Educational journals, trade books, and women's magazines feature articles with such mind-boggling titles as "Advocacy for Gifted and Talented Education" (as opposed to ungifted and untalented education?) and "The Creatively Gifted Child."

Is that last one a notch higher than just plain ol' gifted?

If a rose by any other name smells as sweet, why can't we use the marvelously rich English langauge to come up with a less thorny name for meeting children's different needs with different programs?

What bothers me is the fact that almost every one of our school systems across the nation makes some effort to separate those they label "gifted" from those they label, by insinuation, "not gifted" or "not as gifted" or even "run-of-the-mill, nothing special." Several of the articles I've read have checklists for parents to see if their child is gifted. Or talented.

Does your child love to explore? Does he or she always seem busy? Does she hate playpens? Does he ask a lot of questions?

Then comes the litmus test. Here's how to tell whether your child is gifted, talented and creative: Is his or her IQ above 132?

The Gifted and Talented Education Act of 1978, Section 902, describes "gifted and talented children" as those who are "identified at the preschool, elementary, or secondary level as possessing demonstrated or potential abilities that give evidence in areas such as intellectual, creative, specific academic or leadership ability, or in the performing and visual arts."

Gifted and Talented authorities cite examples from history for us to measure our kids against: Goethe, who by the time he was six was reading Heidegger; Mozart, who was writing music at three; Darwin, who with his plant and shell collections was outclassing everyone else by the time he was eight.

But what about Edison, who was a misfit at school and lasted only a few months? Or Benjamin Franklin, who failed simple arithmetic? Or the Wright brothers, who had no high-school diplomas? Or Edgar Allan Poe, who was pretty much a basket case, certainly not sitting up there in the front row or getting stars by his name.

On the basis of her studies of their childhood, psychologist Catherine Morris Cox says Rembrandt, Copernicus, and Cervantes all had average or below average IQs. Hermann Hesse said, "Creativity is deviant behavior." What about the class clowns and the dropouts? What about the shy kid in the back row whose mind is jumping but who doesn't test well?

Using IQ tests, school grades, and personality traits to decide and then announce whether a child is "gifted" or "has talent" makes about as much sense as putting a pea under the mattress to see if he or she comes from a nice family.

Imagine for a minute that you are a fourth grader. Once or twice a week, the teacher announces that it is "gifted and talented time." So a bunch of kids gather up their books and slip off to do whatever it is that gifted and talented girls and boys do that you can't do because you don't have gifts or talents.

Any educator would be certain and quick to explain that this is, of course, not really what they mean, and I sure hope it isn't. But it must sound that way to any reasonable fourth grader, and people in charge of our children's education should know better than anybody that labels can mess you up for a long time.

It is interesting that Alfred Binet, the French psychologist who developed the intelligence quotient test which is the basis for the IQ test most commonly used today, called his exercises *stunts* and developed the whole scheme as a means of identifying *dull* students rather than smart ones.

Experts tell us that the average IQ is somewhere between 84 and 116. The odds of finding a child with an IQ over 168 are about twenty-eight in a million. Some educators even use the term "severely gifted" for children with IQs above 160. Certainly, children at either extreme require special attention.

We need to find out who they are and make the
necessary provisions for them, try to work with, not
against, their peculiarities and proclivities. That's a
wise educational judgment.

Using the term *gifted* is not a good way to do it.
"Gifted" implies a value, even moral judgment and
is the wrong term to use. All our children are gifted
and talented. That is part of their endowment as human beings. It is the brand name stamped on us all
by our Creator. We should never allow anyone to
talk us out of feeling that way about our children—
or to design a system in which our children themselves decide they might as well hang it up, and get
used to being nothing special.

SPOOKY
QUESTIONS

—๑

"What'ya gonna be for Halloween?"

"Huh?"

"Mom, I don't know what I want to be when I grow up. How do you expect me to worry about what I'm going to be on Halloween?"

It is a problem. Especially when you're ten and just beginning to realize that you're too old for costumes and too young to be satisfied with just answering the door.

Growing pains. When you're a kid—say four, five, six—it's not so earth-shaking. If your mom is a trooper, you can be *anything*. The sky's the limit. She'll sew a clown suit from a Woolworth's pattern, complete with six-inch ruffles and piping around the cuffs. Or, your dad will help you fix a Martian head from an old ice cream container, aluminum-foil antlers, and great big round washers dipped in glitter for the eyes. With your parents' help, you can be a clown or a Martian or a monster or even a magician.

When you're five or six.

But when you're nine or ten, things start getting complicated. Costumes aren't good enough anymore. You begin to realize that life is real; that you've got to decide what you're gonna *be*, and your mom and dad can't make everything fit.

Your teachers tell you to be smart. Your buddies tell you to be cool. Your grandparents tell you to be famous. Your parents tell you to be good. The Bible tells you to be the light of the world, which sounds like a pretty tall order for a ten-year-old. For anybody. Think about it.

Ask any kids under nine, and they'll tell you right off what they want to be when they grow up. A five-year-old doesn't even pause for breath: a teacher; a waitress; a nurse; a fireman; a fighter pilot.

The question is even less complicated during the Age of Wisdom—eight. One eight-year-old I know has it all worked out. He's going to be a star football hero for the Dallas Cowboys. What position?

"Offensive throwback."

But, when you're nine, the realities begin to move

in. You learn that Mom can't fix everything. That Dad doesn't know it all. That it takes more than Legos and Bionic Men and an endless supply of M&M's to make you happy. You begin to figure out that the winos hanging around the bus station were once ten-years-old, too, and certainly didn't plan to become winos. You see your mother trying to find the nerve and the time to take the real-estate exam. You know about your friend's father who drinks because he hates his job. You remember when you were little and wanted to be Kung Fu. Now all that stuff seems pretty silly.

What are you gonna be for Halloween? Well, that's just for one night. A little grease paint, some dime-store fangs, and a blackened-out tooth will take care of that. Or, if worse comes to worse, you can always stay home with your mom and dad and hand out candy corn.

What are you going to be for real?

When you're ten, that's the spooky question.

THE
DIRTY DOZENS

—૭

"Most children at age twelve are in full bloom."

At least that's what it says here in the pamphlet I picked up at the pediatrician's.

Do you have a twelve-year-old? Boy? Then you know exactly what that means. Twelve-year-old boys act like blooming idiots. Twelve is the age of reckoning, and there's no telling what a twelve-year-old boy will reckon to do. There's no logic in his life. Or if there is, it's only his kind.

He can blow up beach rafts, drive his dirt bike off the sliding board, walk up the wall in the back hall, take the steps six at a time, patiently hook together fourteen straws at Hardee's, make complicated masking-tape designs on the den rug, kick the same stone all the way to and from school, paint his radio with plastic model paint—and yet, doesn't have the energy or good sense to brush his hair.

He can stand bootless in a driving rain at his safety-patrol duty, put a whole pack of gum in his mouth at one time, drool into the car lighter and watch it sizzle, go six weeks without a bath, ride roller coasters from dawn to dusk on a hot summer day, eat purple cereal for breakfast—but seven-year-old sisters and leafy vegetables make him sick.

He can't remember where he took off his tennis shoes, but never forgets when it's his turn in the front seat. He grips the spelling book with white fists, groaning over Friday's list—but he can name every make of car since 1955, imitate word for word and voice for voice all the TV commercials, and can argue you blue in the face over why something should be spelled a certain way and furthermore, who says there's only one right way to spell a word anyhow? This is a free country. Weren't people supposed to think for themselves? Wasn't that the point of education?

He considers a shirt dirty when it has spots on both sides; his plate clean when everything's gone but the broccoli legs and the slimy tomatoes; and, by his standards, brushing teeth means sucking off the toothpaste.

He likes his food coated with sugar or drowned in ketchup. His idea of a classic in the world of literature is the *Nintendo Rule Book*, the Time-Life series on sharks, and the backs of cereal boxes. He would go to war to protect his rights to skateboard in the rain, to defend his best friend's reputation, to hold his title as family expert on UFOs, pier fishing, and whatever else is on his mind. Or anybody else's.

He'd absolutely croak if his mother kissed him in public, or if his sister spoke to him in the lunchroom. And he does croak, as a matter of fact, every night, regular as clockwork, when bedtime comes. There's always one more page or program or problem. He never gives up and always goes down in protest, resorting to reading under the covers with a flashlight or building with Legos in the semidarkness.

He's careful to hide his favorite stuffed animals so nobody will think he still has any, his stick deodorant so nobody will think he's using it, the A's on his report card so nobody will think he is smart, his pride in the thickening hair on his legs so nobody will think he has noticed.

He has long conversations with friends about the Dallas Cowboys, ways to earn easy money, how to gross out teachers, who has the meanest parents, and which girls in the class wear a bra.

He speaks softly and tenderly to his new four-month-old cousin, examining each pearl-like toe in newfound amazement. He hollers in a voice that gives his mother hives when he discovers his sister *who-hoo-ing* at him while he's getting undressed, and goes crazy-numb and deaf as a post when asked to take out the trash or tie his shoelaces.

It's an age of reckoning, all right. But somehow, miraculously, mamas reckon they'll hold on to their twelve-year-old just a little longer. Fingers crossed.

Just think. If twelve-year-olds ever got organized, they could take over the world, and we'd all stuff ourselves with peanut butter toast and Mello Yello at four in the afternoon, grow up to hang glide, have terminal cowlicks, and even God would have to hold on to our shirttails to keep up.

THINKING SMALL

—❧

People are always talking about the wonders of childhood—its innocence, the joy, the uncomplicated worldview. *"When I was a child, I spoke as a child . . ."*

We all did.

Some of the words we spoke didn't make sense, but that didn't matter. Children don't have to make sense. I used to lie in bed at night saying aloud words that gradually modulated into yawns and carried me off in a wooden shoe, winking and blinking on a sea of crystal dew to a land where the moon talks.

Of course, it made no sense, but most of us can

still quote those stories from childhood. To children, it is how words sound that give them meaning.

Words were toys back then: *Saskatchewan* . . . *kudzu* . . . *goose liver* . . . *Tchaikovsky* . . .

Who cared what they meant? We just had fun trying them out, listening to how they worked up our throats and out into the silence around us. We were more into sound than sense.

Adults are supposed to make sense, to think things through.

Maybe that's why few adults "sleep like a baby" —the sleep of innocence that has a look all its own. When I can't sleep these days, it never occurs to me to call on Wynken and Blynken, and the only word games I play these days are crossword puzzles in the Sunday paper.

Words aren't toys anymore. They can even be dangerous. Sticks and stones only break bones, but words can kill.

You and I have to work hard to understand each other. It bothers us if somebody tells us we aren't making sense. We could get away with it as children, but as adults, we're held accountable.

Sounding good isn't enough anymore.

"When I was a child, I understood as a child . . ."

I knew money came from the bank, and you got all you wanted, plus a lollypop, if you just stood in line long enough. I understood that being old was wonderful, because you got to drive and stay up late and tell people what to do.

I understood that only people who hated each other fought each other, and only people who loved each other went to church.

"When I was a child, I thought as a child . . ."

I thought babies were cooked in heaven like gingerbread people, and God walked by that heavenly bakery, poking each one of us in the middle, saying, "You're done . . . and you're done . . . and you're done." That's how come we had belly buttons. It's where God poked us.

I thought Santa Claus made it down every chimney in one night, and, for one happy morning, everybody everywhere had everything on their list.

I thought children all over the world ate too much on Thanksgiving and afterward played Monopoly.

And never did it occur to me that there were people in the world who did not get a Valentine from anybody, ever.

If I had known, I would have been sad. But not for long.

When I was a child, my prayers floated up to heaven just like there was no roof, and I sat in the pew on Sunday morning and drew pictures during the sermon while my mother tickled my arm. I never had first—much less second or third—thoughts about anything I heard, or felt a single pang of sin or shame.

When I was a child, I thought people you loved never did anything to hurt you, and they always loved you back, and they never went away.

I thought the world stopped at the end of my driveway and began with warm, pink sunlight smiling through white eyelet curtains.

"But, when I became a man, I put away childish things."

There's only one thing worse, I suppose, than not ever having known the joys of childhood—the innocent, simple view of things. And that is not ever having given them up.

The world can't be run on make-believe.

We need to put away childish things.

But, if you really want to know the truth, sometimes I'd like to have them back.

TO WHOM
IT MAY
CONCERN

—͡ꝰ

Wouldn't it be nice if a mom could send her child out into the world with a list of instructions and a guarantee? The day they set out for kindergarten, all slicked up in a new outfit and carrying shiny new lunch boxes, if we mothers who smile and sniff back at the bus stop had our "druthers," we'd send along a letter that goes something like this:

To Whom It May Concern, and I Sure Hope It Does:

This is a very special little five-year-old girl. She is especially special to her father, who is still mumbling incoherently about where all the time has gone.

182

It seems like only yesterday when she spent her mornings flopping around in my shoes and watching *Captain Kangaroo*. However, if you know a few important things about her, I am sure she will love school as much as I did a hundred years ago.

Whenever she gets hurt or upset, she gets a stomach ache. The best remedy is to put her on your lap and kiss her three times—on the cheek, neck, and forehead. Just a little family ritual perhaps you should know about. She likes to be called Snicklefritz, her daddy's pet name for her, which might come in handy if she gets homesick.

As for lunch, she doesn't like spinach, squash, asparagus, cooked carrots, yams (only sweet potatoes with marshmallows), beets, veal, or potato salad. She likes hot dogs (no mustard), hamburgers (with mayonnaise), soup (Campbell's Chicken & Stars), pizza (plain), and peanut butter (not the generic kind and never crunchy). Please add a teaspoon of sugar to her milk or else she will make a horrible face and may spit it out.

Her lunch money will be in a little purse around her neck. She knows her quarters from her nickels, but dimes give her a fit. Just remind her a dime is the thing she swallowed once. If she ever should lose her money, please don't let her go hungry. We have MasterCard and Visa.

She forgets sometimes that she needs to go to the bathroom, but you can usually tell by the way she stands. She doesn't like to wash her hands before lunch, so will you patiently remind her about ten times?

Should there ever be a thunderstorm during school, please hold her hand and make jokes about how the angels must be bowling in heaven. I know that's not very scientific, but it helps. You'll probably need to comb her hair every day after recess. Please use only covered rubber bands, and I'm sure you can tell that it looks better parted on the left.

She's very worried about carrying her own lunch tray without the food sliding off, and about finding my car after school. So, would you carry her tray for, say, the first six months? My car is a green Dodge, and there will be a dog waiting in it with me.

She has several special talents perhaps you should know about. For instance, she made up a cute little song about a bumble bee. If you ever could use it, I am sure her father would be delighted to come do the background buzzing. She can make French toast in her Easy-Bake oven, get to fifteen doing the lemon twist, and recently wrote a poem about "Giggley, the Wiggley Worm," which might be nice for the school paper.

If you will remember these few things about our Precious Angel, I am sure she will be your favorite student, destined to fame in the Red Robin Reading

Group, the Talent Development Program, the Safety Patrol and, eventually, Phi Beta Kappa.

Should you need me, don't hesitate to call: 373-0689 (home); 332-5123 (office); 375-3969 (next door); 352-8197 (her dad's office); 382-1763 (the grocery store where I shop, just in case); 387-5211 (where Dad eats lunch); or 374-2221 (police).

I'll be happy to come sit in the desk with her, if you ever need me.

P.S. Please don't make her grow up too fast. We like her just the way she is!